The Pocket Guide to
Trusts & Estates

Understanding
Estate Planning, Estate Settlement,
Estate Litigation,
Asset Protection, and Elder Law

By
William E. Andersen, J.D., LL.M., AEP®
James W. Collins, J.D.
Joleen Searles, J.D., LL.M.
Julie Ann Garber, J.D.
With
Paralegals Erin L. Turner and Jerry Saresky, FRP

Throughout this book, hypothetical examples are used to illustrate various planning techniques. These are not representative of any specific situation. Your results will vary. The authors and publishers of this book are not engaged in rendering legal, tax, accounting, insurance, financial and investment planning, or similar professional services in the pages of this book. While legal, tax, accounting, insurance, and financial planning educational topics covered in this book have been checked with sources believed to be reliable, some material may be affected by changes in the laws or in the interpretations of such laws, since the manuscript for this book was completed. For that reason, the accuracy and completeness of such information and the opinions based thereon are not guaranteed. Tax laws are subject to constant change, so financial figures used in this book are for illustrative purposes only, and apply to laws in effect at the time of publication. Check with your professional advisors to determine the current tax laws. In addition, state or local tax laws or procedural rules may have a material impact on the general educational recommendations made by the authors, and the strategies outlined in this book may not be suitable for every individual or every situation. If legal, tax, accounting, insurance, investment, financial planning, or other expert advice is required, obtain the services of a competent licensed practitioner.

Copyright © 2013 "Second Edition" by The Andersen Firm, A Professional Corporation. All rights reserved. No part of this book may be reproduced or used in any form or by any means, electronic or mechanical, including photocopying, recording, or any information or retrieval system, without the prior written permission of the publisher.

ISBN 978-1-4675-3691-2

Collaborative Press, LLC
Omaha, NE

Printed in the USA

What Others Say

This book is rich with valuable information essential to families and professionals engaged in estate planning. Much in the same manner as Bill Andersen guided our family through the process of assuring the preservation of our wealth for our children and grandchildren, this book makes a daunting subject matter easy to understand, and makes use of the most innovative and enduring tax and accounting tools available.

Nicholas L. Trivisonno
Chairman and Chief Executive Officer (Retired)
ACNielsen Corporation

Over the course of my career, I have helped change the way consumers make purchases. Likewise, this guide explains in a very direct and easy to understand manner how to financially plan appropriately for both business and family. It is a must read in today's challenging financial climate.

Ruth Ann Marshall
President of the Americas, MasterCard International, 1996-2006
Board of Directors for Regions Financial Corporation,
ConAgra, Pella Windows
Named one of "The 100 Most Powerful Women" by Forbes Magazine

One of the things I write about and teach is how to cast with a fly rod with maximum efficiency. The authors of this book have captured the fundamentals of estate planning to advanced techniques in a clear and comprehensive manner that is easy for the lay person to understand. This is just a must-have book.

Lefty Kreh
Outdoor Writer, Author, Photographer and Instructor
IGFA Hall of Fame Lifetime Achievement Award

Few books come along these days which equal this. Well thought out and impressively detailed, the reader can understand estate planning in a short period of time thereby laying aside the elemental struggle between fear and action.

Jeffrey Cardenas, Pulitzer Prize Nominee
Author of *Sea Level* and *Marquesa*
Founder, *Salt Water Angler*

How refreshing – technically astute professionals who communicate in words an ordinary human being can understand! This book illuminates estate planning like never before. From introduction to end, the focus on taking care of loved ones in a most professional and fiscally responsible manner jumps out at the reader. Very easy to understand.

Lawrence J. Kendzior, CPA/ABV
Author of *Conundrum: The Challenge of Execution in Middle-Market Companies*

The Pocket Guide to Trusts and Estates is a good example of highly rated professionals explaining ideas in a way that non-lawyers can easily understand. This will be a handbook for me and my team as we explain these concepts to our clients. This book will be around for years to come.

R. Lynn Shipley, Jr.
Chairman and Chief Executive Officer
TriSummit Bank

Wow! Bill Andersen fully explains the "whys" of comprehensive estate planning for financial advisors and clients! This is easy to understand and grasp. Finally. I'll be handing out this book to all my friends and family.

Martin Hirsch
President, Barjon Investments, LLC

This is a one-of-a-kind book. Bill has a gift for making arcane tax law understandable for the common client. This handbook should be in every estate planner's library and given to every client engaged in estate planning.

Benjamin L. Platt, CPA, MBA, CFF, CVA
Managing Partner
Kresge, Platt & Abare, CPAs

FOREWORD

It is difficult to overstate the importance of estate, financial, and asset protection planning to the American family, and yet such planning is still neglected by the vast majority. Why is that?

Some people think planning is only for "the rich." But estate planning is really for everyone who loves family and friends. Others think that it's only about death, and therefore a negative topic. But planning is equally about keeping control of your wealth, and providing for yourself and those you love throughout your lifetime.

Still others think the whole planning topic is just too complex – and they don't have time to figure it all out. It's for this last group that this book is especially written. Although there are several moving parts in the planning process, they are logically consistent with the goal of estate planning. That goal for most people is to:

- Maintain control of what I own while I'm alive and well

- Take care of me and my loved ones if I'm disabled

- When I'm gone, be sure that my wealth goes to the people I want, when I want, and in the way I want

- Accomplish all this with the least amount of stress, and in a way that will keep my family together, and not cause divisions.

Attorneys Bill Andersen, Jim Collins, and Joleen Searles are old friends and colleagues of mine, and partners in The Andersen Firm, an AV Preeminent rated national law firm that focuses on estate planning, estate settlement, estate litigation, asset protection, and elder law. The authors are well-known throughout the country as expert planners. They are practitioners and educators known for their ability to clearly explain complex issues and keep it interesting. I've asked them to make an important contribution to our understanding of estate planning by creating this "pocket guide" to the topic.

Our request was to keep it as simple as possible. It's not a law school course. The goal is that you can read the relevant parts of this little book in a couple of hours, and have a good basic understanding of what you need to do. If nothing else, be sure to read the summary boxes within each chapter! My hope for you is that this book goes beyond education, and motivates you to take action on these important matters for the people you love and the causes you care about.

Daniel P. Stuenzi, JD
Publisher
Collaborative Press, LLC

The Pocket Guide to Trusts & Estates

Understanding Estate Planning, Estate Settlement, Estate Litigation, Asset Protection, and Elder Law

What Others Say

Foreword

PART ONE – BASIC PLANNING

1. **Do It Early** 1
   Some of the most intelligent, motivated, and successful people are simply irresponsible when it comes to estate planning, estate settlement, estate litigation, asset protection, and elder law

2. **Estate Planning from 30,000 Feet: The Fabulous Four** 7
   a. Foundational Planning (The Basics)
   b. Retirement Planning (IRAs)
   c. Tax Planning (Federal and State)
   d. Asset Protection Planning (During and After Life...On Shore and Offshore)

3. **The Essential Players** 9
   A few minutes with key advisors in person, on a conference call, or by email can make the difference between a plan that works and one that doesn't

4. **Wills are Wrong.** 11
   The only one who wins with a will is the lawyer

Table of Contents

5. **Avoiding Probate: Don't Tell it to the Judge** 13
   How to avoid throwing your money away and making an unpleasant experience your final gift to your loved ones

6. **The 7 Mandatory Components of a Foundational Estate Plan** ... 15
   The basics that everyone needs

7. **The Revocable Living Trust (RLT)** 19
   The foundational document for most estate plans

8. **Properly Titling Your Assets (Funding Your Estate Plan)** 21
   "Cleaning the dishes after Thanksgiving dinner"

9. **Choosing Trustees.** 25
   Individual(s) or Institution(s) – or a combination of the two

10. **Duties of a Trustee** 27
    What you and your trustees should know before agreeing to serve

11. **What Do I Do With My Stuff?** 31
    How to keep the kids from fighting over your personal property

12. **Mental Disability Planning** 33
    Don't put your family through a guardianship proceeding

13. **Planning for IRAs, 401(k)s, and other Retirement Money** 37
    The IRA Inheritance Trust will protect it and let it grow income tax-deferred

14. **Federal and State Estate Taxes.** 43
    Quantifying the taxes, hoping for the best, but planning for the worst

15. **How Do I Calculate My Federal and Local Estate Tax.** 45
    Just call us and we'll tell you the current temperature and today's forecast – if you don't like the weather, just wait and it may get better (or worse)

16. **Estate, Gift, and Income Tax Planning** 47
    You only have 6 choices, and one of them is to pay the tax

Table of Contents

17. **Where You Live Matters** 49
    Avoid state inheritance and estate taxes, and win a second home

18. **Insurance and the Irrevocable Life Insurance Trust (ILIT)** 51
    Using insurance to pay part or all of the estate, inheritance, and income tax, while keeping the value of the insurance out of your estate

19. **Buying Insurance** 57
    Use an advisor who is a knowledgeable insurance professional, not a salesman

PART TWO – ADVANCED PLANNING

20. **Advanced Planning Techniques** 61
    When you don't want to give it to the government and insurance is not the (total) answer

21. **The Grantor Deemed Owner Trust (GDOT)** 65
    How to buy insurance and not incur gift taxes

22. **Buildup Equity Retirement Trusts (BERTs)** 69
    A gift for your spouse – protecting the asset, removing the value from your estate, and providing for your beneficiaries

23. **Qualified Personal Residence Trusts (QPRTs)** 73
    Remove the value of your home from your estate, protect it, and live in it just as you do now

24. **Uniform Trust to Minors Accounts (UTMAs)** 77
    A word to the wise – do not use them

25. **Legacy Trusts** 81
    Gifting to the children, grandchildren, and others while providing asset protection and maintaining some control (if you want to)

26. **Grantor Retained Annuity Trusts (GRATs)** 85
    One way to gift appreciating assets to the kids (or others) – but do it sooner rather than later

Table of Contents

27. **Self-Cancelling Installment Notes (SCINs)** 89
    Another way to pass money to the next generation with minimal taxes

28. **The Advantages of Being a U.S. Citizen in Estate Planning** 93
    Be aware of the planning pitfalls if you (or your spouse) are not a U.S. citizen

29. **Asset Protection** 99
    Keeping it in the family after you're gone

30. **Asset Protection – Domestic Techniques** 103
    Why leave yourself unprotected during life – penny wise and dollar foolish

31. **Asset Protection – Offshore Techniques** 111
    Avoiding the uncertainties of U.S. courts

32. **The Secret of Discounts for Gifting** 115
    The "Freeze & Squeeze" technique

33. **Divorce and Estate Planning** 119
    The pitfalls of divorce, separation, and beneficiary designations

34. **Charitable Planning** 123
    If you have a charitable passion there are many choices on how to give

35. **Direct Gifts to Charity** 127
    Beware of the downside to both your money and the charity

36. **Charitable Annuity Trusts and Unitrusts** 129
    Ways to provide for the kids, give to charity, and save taxes

37. **Private Foundations** 135
    Only if you're leaving $1 million or more to charity, and have a person with a charitable passion as strong as your own

38. **Community Foundations and Donor Advised Funds** 137
    How to "borrow" a 501(c)(3) charitable organization with the same results at a much lower cost – and you can include your family in decision-making

Table of Contents

39. **Charitable Annuities** **141**
    If you are giving to the "Big Boys" it can make a lot of sense

40. **Business Succession Planning** **143**
    You need to have a plan if you want your business to continue when you're disabled or deceased

41. **Buy-Sell Agreements** **147**
    If you are in business with someone else, and the business is important to you or your family, you need one

42. **Planning for Same Sex and Unwed Couples** **151**
    Planning for couples who are "unmarried" is not the same as planning for two people who are "single" or in a legally recognized marriage

43. **Special Needs Trusts** **155**
    Don't jump too quickly because this may not be right for your situation

44. **Long Term Care Insurance** **159**
    Is it right for you – or do you have sufficient assets to self-insure

45. **Elder Law** **161**
    It is vital to plan earlier rather than later

46. **The "Inheriting Trust"** **165**
    How to talk to Mom and Dad about their estate plan

47. **Estate Settlement** **169**
    Even with a trust there are things that need to be done after you're gone (but nowhere near as bad as probate)

48. **Avoiding Estate Litigation: Death, Greed, and Money** ... **173**
    The lawyers win and the children hate each other

49. **What Type of Estate Plan is Right for You?** **177**
    The "cookie cutter" approach doesn't work

50. **The Cost of Estate Planning** **179**
    You get what you pay for

Table of Contents

Acknowledgements 183

APPENDIX A – Author Biographies 185

APPENDIX B – Summary of Key Ideas 193

PART ONE

Basic Planning

CHAPTER 1

Do It Early

Some of the most intelligent, motivated, and successful people are simply irresponsible when it comes to estate planning, estate settlement, estate litigation, asset protection, and elder law

The estates of famous people often make the news, and usually not to highlight how good their planning was, but rather because of complications that arise after their death. What you don't hear about in the news are all the other smart and successful people who are not celebrities, but whose families also have big problems after they pass away.

In the last few decades, it seems that the owners of NFL football teams have especially been plagued by poor planning. Here are some examples.

Miami Dolphins

The estate tax problems for owners of the Miami Dolphins started with the Robbie family, the namesake of the Joe Robbie Stadium. The Dolphins were sold by the Robbie family to Wayne Huizenga in 1994 because the surviving family members could not pay the estimated $50 million in estate taxes required to keep the team.

One week prior to Huizenga's 70th birthday, an inside source said, "He's got a big estate-planning problem. If [Huizenga] were to die while in possession of the Dolphins, the IRS would appraise the team, and Huizenga's heirs could be

CHAPTER 1 Do It Early

stuck with a $450-plus million bill to cover estate taxes. Huizenga's tax share on a sale of the team would be much lower, roughly $114 million. The team and the stadium are Wayne's only liquid assets."

In early 2008, Huizenga agreed to sell 50% of the team to New York real estate developer Stephen Ross, and by the end of that year, ended up selling 95% of the Dolphins, the stadium, and 50% of the surrounding developable land to Ross. Huizenga said that he hoped to "close on the deal by early January to ensure that the capital gains taxes on the sale remain at 15 percent before a new President takes over."

Washington Redskins

Jack Cooke started business as a door-to-door encyclopedia salesman, and grew until he owned a collection of sports teams, real estate, and other assets valued at more than $1 billion. Most know him as the former owner of the Washington Redskins football team. Although a successful and sophisticated businessman, his estate planning failed miserably.

The problems started with Cooke's approach to estate planning which apparently was not based on extensive counseling and a comprehensive plan. For example, Cooke had a basic will – and that will had been amended eight times. It left seven executors, most of whom were former employees who had never seen the will, never knew its instructions, and in some cases, never knew they had been appointed.

Cooke was married, and then divorced, and then remarried to the same woman. Upon the second marriage, his wife signed a prenuptial agreement which waived her claim to his estate. Nevertheless, after his death, she brought a lawsuit which resulted in a $10 million settlement to her and $6.8 million in legal costs to the estate.

Another problem was the disagreement between executors Stuart Haney and Jack Cooke, Jr. over the Jack Kent Cooke Foundation. The foundation had been established to help underprivileged students, but due to the large estate tax bill, the only way the foundation could be funded was to sell some of the assets of the estate. Haney wanted to sell the Washington Redskins, but Cooke, Jr.

disagreed. Cooke's son had worked in management of the Redskins for most of his life, shared his father's passion for football and for the team, and dreamed of someday becoming the owner. Jack Cooke, Jr. insisted that the Redskins franchise not pass from family control and wanted to instead sell the Chrysler building in New York City to pay the taxes.

The Chrysler Building, however, was losing $1.5 million a month and its market value didn't come close to the loans against it. The executors, therefore, with the exception of Cooke, Jr., chose to auction the Redskins team. The team went to Daniel Snyder for a bid of $800 million.

The next fight was how much the executors should be paid for their work because the estate plan (the will) did not specify an amount. The court decided to award the state's statutory 5% fee, which equaled approximately $37.6 million – again reducing the size of the inheritance for the family. In the end, Cooke, Jr. never received the Redskins, and the executors disliked one another, yet they still had to work together as they were all named on the board of directors for the Foundation. Eventually, $64 million was spent on professional fees

Oakland Raiders

At the time of his death in 2011, a lot of people who knew Al Davis were speculating that his estate could potentially face big inheritance taxes based on the value of the Oakland Raiders. Davis bought a 10% interest in the Oakland Raiders for $18,500 in 1966 and increased his stake to 67% over the years. In 2007 he sold 20% of the team for $150 million, leaving himself in control of 47%. At the time of his death, the Raiders were calculated to be worth $761 million –potentially causing hundreds of millions of dollars in estate taxes.

In the days following Davis' death, several sources in the media quoted team chief executive Amy Trask as saying that Davis used thorough estate and succession planning to keep the Oakland Raiders in the family. The planning accounted for estate taxes, and no sale of the team would be required.

It is quite possible that Davis made use of the "unlimited marital deduction" to pass the team to his wife, Carol, thus avoiding all estate taxes – for now. The big concern for Raiders' fans and the city of Oakland is what will happen when

Carol passes away. It's no secret that the NFL would rather have the team back in Los Angeles, and that could more easily be accomplished with a new owner. Unless Carol too has done some very comprehensive estate planning – most likely including large sums to charity and the purchase of very large insurance policies – only a small part of the value of the team will be exempted from taxes when it passes to Al and Carol's son, Mark – and that's when the team may have to be sold.

> You tried to be responsible during your life. Don't be irresponsible at the end.

But I'm Not an NFL Team Owner!

Of course, these examples are illustrative of the worst case scenarios and very large amounts of money. But every year in America, thousands of small business owners and farm families are impacted in the exact same way, although with less money involved. The amount of taxes owed is unimportant when you're forced to sell your family business or your family farm to pay those taxes. It's especially painful when your children were counting on that business or farm for their livelihood, and hoped to pass it on someday to your grandchildren.

The good news is that by starting early, and planning well, these heartaches can be avoided.

CHAPTER 2

Estate Planning from 30,000 Feet: The Fabulous Four

Before we get into the details of planning, it's probably helpful to first take a look at the big picture. We tend to think of planning at two levels: basic and advanced. Basic planning is the type needed by everyone who owns anything and who cares about anyone. Advanced planning covers special situations such as large taxable estates, business ownership, asset protection concerns, and special needs beneficiaries. Those clients who need advanced planning must first complete the basic planning, and build from that foundation.

All of the planning topics and tools covered in this Pocket Guide will first be classified as either basic or advanced. Then, each topic and tool can be further classified under one of the four general categories described below.

Foundational Planning

Every client needs foundational planning. This will include the seven mandatory components that provide structure to the overall plan: a revocable living trust, pour-over will, financial power of attorney, health care surrogate, living will, quitclaim bill of sale, and a funding plan. Each of these components is described in more detail in the pages that follow.

CHAPTER 2 Estate Planning from 30,000 Feet: The Fabulous Four

Retirement Planning

Retirement planning will deal with your personal retirement plans such as IRAs and Roth IRAs, as well as employer-provided plans such as 401(k) and 403(b) plans. With proper planning, the tax benefits of these plans can be extended well beyond your lifetime.

Tax Planning

Tax planning comes in a wide variety of techniques that can be employed to reduce income, gift, inheritance, and/or estate taxes – depending on your specific situation and goals. In Chapter 16 you'll learn that you really only have six planning options and only one of them is to pay the tax! For affluent clients facing large estate tax problems, there are at least 60 sophisticated planning techniques that can be implemented to reduce or eliminate those taxes. Several of the most common techniques are explained in later chapters.

> You need to ask your attorney about the "Fabulous Four": Foundational Planning, Retirement Planning, Tax Planning, and Asset Protection

Asset Protection Planning

Asset protection planning can be employed both to protect your current assets, and to protect the inheritance that you leave to your loved ones. We will explore methods for protecting assets both simple and complex, both domestically and offshore.

CHAPTER 3

The Essential Players

A few minutes in person or on a conference call can make the difference between a plan that works and one that doesn't

One of the key components to an estate plan that works is the involvement of a team of essential participants, including both professional advisors and family members.

When it comes to professional advisors, the key players are your estate planning attorney, your financial advisor, your CPA, and your insurance advisor. If you own a business, you will probably also want to include your business attorney.

Each advisor plays a crucial role in an effective and successful plan, and only through cooperation and collaboration will your plan be the best it can be. You may have had occasion to receive advice from one of your advisors that was at odds with the advice of a second advisor. Perhaps your financial advisor recommends one course of action, but your attorney disagrees. Or your attorney recommends a particular plan, but your CPA tells you it won't work. Few things are more frustrating. Which expert do you trust?

The thoughtful approach is to involve all the advisors you care to include in your planning. Only when all the advisors are working together to implement and maintain your plan, will they be on the same page and in complete agreement. And only through that approach will the plan work the way you intend.

Other essential players are typically members of your family. They may be given your Power of Attorney or be named as your Health Care Surrogate. They often

CHAPTER 3 The Essential Players

serve as Trustees or Trust Protectors. These important helpers must be aware of your plan and their designated role. They should know ahead of time what is expected of them, and you should have confidence that they are ready and willing to participate.

> Good advisors play well in the "sand box" with one another.

One final group that may be involved in planning is your beneficiaries. This, of course, is up to you as the client. Some families are more open than others with the children and grandchildren on financial matters and future planning. But ongoing communication about these issues can be important to preserving the unity of the family after you are gone. If it is difficult for you to discuss these topics, your attorney and other advisors can help.

CHAPTER 4

Wills are Wrong

The only one who wins with a will is the lawyer

The funny thing about wills is that they often don't accomplish your will! In our foundational planning, we use an instrument called a pour-over will. This is different than the simple Last Will and Testament that is prescribed by many attorneys. The pour-over will is tied to a revocable living trust, and is used to pick up any "loose ends" that may have been missed in the planning, and tie them to the comprehensive instructions within the trust.

Here are a few problems with planning your estate using only a will:

- A will is a death instrument. It can't do anything for you while you're alive. It just sits there in your safe deposit box waiting for your demise.

- A will only controls assets that are titled in your name alone. It does not control jointly owned property, life insurance policies, or retirement accounts.

- A will cannot help if you become mentally disabled. Again, it doesn't do anything while you're alive.

> Wills are wrong! Not illegal... just stupid!

- A will goes through a legal process called probate which is described in the next chapter. Sometimes the biggest beneficiary of the will is the attorney who receives the probate legal fees!

- A will distributes assets without protections and without instructions for your heirs.

We typically recommend the use of a Revocable Living Trust (described in Chapter 7) as the central document for our clients' estate plans. The trust is a lifetime instrument that avoids all the problems and challenges of the will alone.

CHAPTER 5

Avoiding Probate: Don't Tell it to the Judge

How to avoid throwing your money away and making your final gift to your loves ones an unpleasant experience

When we explore clients' motivations for planning, we often hear "I want to avoid probate." When we pursue that idea further, we learn that the client doesn't really know what probate is, but they've heard enough about it to know that probate is "bad" and everyone wants to avoid it!

Probate is a court proceeding that is used to carry out the instructions in a Last Will and Testament. And while the procedure varies from state to state, we agree with those who say that it should be avoided if at all possible. There are several reasons for this.

First of all, since probate takes place in court before a judge, it is a matter of public record. In recent years, new laws and a whole industry have been developed to protect your privacy. Why should those protections end when you die? You probably don't say a lot publicly about your private financial matters, so why would you want the details available to a nosy neighbor or a predator after you're gone? Plus, a public record and court hearing makes the will easy to contest by disgruntled relatives.

Another inherent problem with probate (as with any court proceeding) is that it typically involves lawyers – most of whom charge fees. In some states, the fee

CHAPTER 5　Avoiding Probate: Don't Tell it to the Judge

charged can be substantial. Why have your loved ones pay fees that could be easily avoided with proper planning?

A third problem is that the probate process can be time-consuming. Court dockets are often over-crowded and just getting scheduled to see a judge may take awhile. And when you finally get a court date, it is common for the judge to require more information. Missing paperwork and ownership records need to be tracked down, and new hearings scheduled. The process can drag on for months, and in many cases, even years.

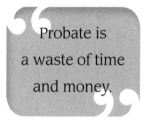

"Probate is a waste of time and money."

So how can you avoid probate and its attendant problems altogether? Consider the use of a fully funded revocable living trust as described in the pages that follow.

CHAPTER 6

The 7 Mandatory Components of a Foundational Estate Plan

The basics that everyone needs

1. Revocable Living Trust

This instrument contains in-depth instructions for your care and the care of your loved ones if you become mentally disabled, and upon your death. Furthermore, it efficiently transfers your property to your loved ones at the time of your death, avoiding probate and allowing for the maximum utilization of estate tax exemptions.

2. Pour-Over Will

Upon your death, your "pour-over will" transfers any property to your living trust that you did not put into it before your death. It functions as a safety net to make sure property you neglected to place in your trust can ultimately be managed by your Trustees according to your instructions.

3. Durable Power of Attorney

A durable power of attorney allows someone else to handle financial matters for assets in your individual name, including retirement plans. It is also used to put assets in your trust if you become mentally disabled prior to your trust becoming fully funded.

4. Living Will

This instrument directs your physician as to whether or not to cease life-sustaining procedures which would serve only to prolong your death if you are terminally ill. It gives guidelines for your physician to follow, as well as clarifies your specific intent as to life-sustaining procedures.

5. Health Care Surrogate /Health Care Power of Attorney

This instrument designates a health care surrogate or health care power of attorney if you are incapable of making health care decisions or providing informed consent. It must also conform to HIPAA (the Health Insurance Portability and Accountability Act of 1996) to be effective.

6. Quitclaim Bill of Sale

This instrument places your personal property (e.g. furniture and jewelry) into your trust, thus avoiding the need to probate your personal property.

7. Funding

Most assets will need to be re-titled into the trust to make the trust effective for disability planning and to avoid probate. Funding a trust is just as important as creating the trust.

> **If you don't have the 7 mandatory components of a Foundational Estate Plan, you don't have a proper estate plan.**

CHAPTER 6   The 7 Mandatory Components of a Foundational Estate Plan

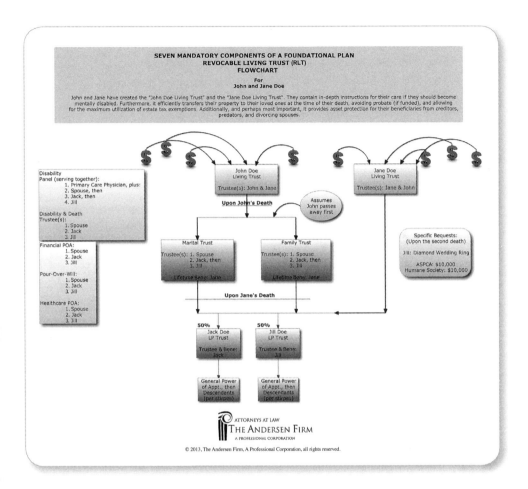

CHAPTER 7

The Revocable Living Trust (RLT)

The foundational document for most estate plans

The revocable living trust acts as a will substitute and contains instructions for managing your assets during your life and also upon death. A living trust is created during your lifetime and becomes effective immediately when you sign it. After a trust is created, your assets should be transferred into the name of your trust. That process is called "funding."

You can transfer property to the trust, and still maintain control and use of all the property during your lifetime. You can revoke or change the trust at any time. You can be the trustee of your trust (or co-trustee with your spouse), and because these transfers are made ahead of time, a successor trustee that you choose can step into your shoes if you become mentally disabled, or die. That successor trustee can immediately start handling your financial affairs without a court order or the need to establish a guardianship or conservatorship.

> Do not leave your wealth outright or staggered at different ages, or it will not be protected for your loved ones.

Revocable living trusts may be used to avoid the probate process upon death. But to achieve that objective, the trust must be fully "funded" with your assets during lifetime, since assets

CHAPTER 7   The Revocable Living Trust (RLT)

left in your own name will most likely have to go through probate. When we create a revocable living trust, we also create a "pour-over will" to catch any forgotten assets after death. Even a pour-over will must go through probate, but it should be faster and less expensive, and most importantly, those forgotten assets will still be handled according to your specific trust instructions.

If you are married, the revocable living trust may provide for the creation of a marital trust and family trust upon the death of the first spouse. You'll sometimes hear these referred to as "A and B Trusts." These "subtrusts" are designed to both maximize a married couple's total estate tax exemptions, and to protect the trust assets against the surviving spouse's "creditors and predators" – which may include a new spouse should the surviving spouse remarry. 2012 tax legislation (ATRA 2012) made permanent a tool first temporarily introduced under 2010 tax law known as "portability," which allows the estate of the first deceased spouse to elect to file a Form 706 estate tax purpose in order to pass any "deceased spouse unused exemption" to the surviving spouse. However, there are many intricacies with portability to consider, and it is very often poor advice to depend on portability alone rather than using the standard A and B Trusts. Portability is not a panacea.

After both spouses have died, assets may be distributed to the couple's children or other beneficiaries in a variety of ways – including:

- immediate outright distributions (WRONG!)
- staggered distributions at various ages (WRONG!)
- lifetime trusts with liberal or conservative standards (RIGHT!)
- or special needs trusts. (SOMETIMES)

Many of our clients choose to pass the inheritance into new trusts for their children that will also provide ongoing creditor and predator protections for future generations.

CHAPTER 8

Properly Titling Your Assets (Funding Your Estate Plan)

"Cleaning the dishes after Thanksgiving dinner"

We use the experience of a Thanksgiving Day dinner to help you remember the importance of funding. There are many steps that go into preparing and serving a great Thanksgiving dinner. In our analogy, the counseling, design, and drafting of your estate plan is the "cooking" phase of the dinner. When we implement the plan and put all of your entities into effect that is like the "eating" phase. But the Thanksgiving meal isn't really done until somebody cleans up from the meal and does the dishes! In the estate planning process, we call that funding the plan. And like the Thanksgiving dinner dishes, it's the least fun part of the whole process. Nevertheless, it's crucial to the success of your plan!

Funding is simply the act of transferring your assets to your revocable living trust. If you create a living trust but never get around to funding the trust, your unfunded assets will not be controlled by the trust instructions. At best, the unfunded assets will be transferred by use of a "pour-over will." But after-death funding generally requires that your pour-over will be probated so that your executor will have legal authority to transfer your assets to your trust.

CHAPTER 8   Properly Titling Your Assets (Funding Your Estate Plan)

Since most people establish trusts with the expectation that their estate will not require probate, the pour-over will should only be used as a last resort.

And even with a pour-over will you can't be sure that all of your assets will make it into your trust after death. Most married people with unfunded trusts own their assets with a spouse as joint owners with rights of survivorship. That means that the assets will not pass to the trust, or be controlled by a pour-over will, but will instead pass automatically to the surviving owner.

Funding is not a difficult task, but it requires attention to detail and persistence. It requires you to notify all of your financial institutions in writing of the proposed change. Most of the time, at least one follow-up communication is required to ensure that proper titling takes place.

You can take the steps to fund your trust yourself. However, many clients start out with good intentions, but end up never completing their funding. When an advisor checks on the funding process a month or two later, they typically hear the client say, "Remind me what funding is again," or "We've been meaning to get started on that." The biggest enemies of proper funding are procrastination and frustration. Your professional advisors should have processes in place to help ensure you complete your funding properly.

> If you do not have a specific written plan on how to title assets, and the required documents with which to do it, you need to get them immediately.

Some clients are concerned that if a major change occurs in their trust plan that they will have to create a brand new trust, and go through the whole funding process over again. However, you can simply "restate" your trust, acknowledging the creation of your trust on the date you originally created it, and stating that you wish to restate that trust in its entirety. The restated contents of the trust will take the place of the contents of your old trust, but the trust name doesn't change.

One of the biggest mistakes made by estate planning attorneys is to draft a bunch of documents, but never take the time to ensure that assets are titled in

CHAPTER 8   Properly Titling Your Assets (Funding Your Estate Plan)

such a way that the plan actually controls the assets! Any good funding plan should include:

- a list of your assets and how they are currently titled,
- instructions on how each should be titled to fit with the plan,
- documents that are necessary to make the required changes in title, and
- clear assignments between you, your attorney, and your other advisors as to who is responsible to see that each change is accomplished.

CHAPTER 9

Choosing Trustees

Individuals or institutions – or a combination of the two

The trustee's job includes a focus on accounting, investment, and tax matters. The trustee must evaluate the needs of the beneficiaries, exercise good judgment to hire the right advisors, and follow the terms of the trust agreement. Choosing a trustee requires thought and consideration. The responsibility given a trustee is serious and can last for many years. The trustee plays a critical role in the management of the trust assets.

All trusts require at least one trustee. Depending on the type of trust involved, the trustmaker may initially act as trustee as in a revocable living trust. If you are married when you first create a trust, you and your spouse will typically serve as co-trustees in both trusts. At death, the surviving spouse, children, a trusted friend, or a professional entity (such as a bank or trust company) may serve as successor trustee. One of the most important decisions in choosing a trustee is whether to use an individual or a professional entity.

Many people choose a family member such as a surviving spouse, child, or other relative to serve as trustee. The benefit is that the family member typically has a personal stake in seeing the trust succeed and grow. A family member is more likely to know the beneficiaries and their individual circumstances, thus being able to make more informed personal decisions. And, family members often serve without charging a fee for their services.

CHAPTER 9 Choosing Trustees

However, some trusts require a high level of expertise to manage the trust assets or require a lot of time to deal with the beneficiaries. Family members may lack the financial acumen to manage trust assets and may need the services of financial advisors, accountants, and attorneys in carrying out trustee duties. This may offset or exceed the savings derived from choosing a family member in the first place. Furthermore, family members may not be able to distance themselves so as to act impartially among beneficiaries.

> "The trustee is in control. You serve first, and then you choose who replaces you."

The corporate trustee, on the other hand, will typically be impartial, and will have expertise in trust investment and management. They also tend, however, to be more impersonal than a friend or family member – not really knowing or caring about the circumstances of specific beneficiaries.

If a trust is anticipated to last for a long time, it is important to choose a number of successor trustees or to appoint people who can name successor trustees, in the event any of them cannot act. A bank or corporate trustee can usually serve for generations.

There is also the option of choosing a mix of trustees, to include both family members and professional entities. Quite often, the corporate trustee is chosen to handle trust investments and financial or tax issues, while the family trustee deals with the beneficiaries, including conflicts between beneficiaries, or discretionary choices based on a beneficiary's behavior. If you choose multiple trustees, it is important that you specify in the trust agreement how disputes between the various trustees will be solved, and who has the ultimate decision-making power.

CHAPTER 10

Duties of a Trustee

What you and your trustees should know before agreeing to serve

Depending on the type of trust and beneficiaries, a Trustee's job is a major responsibility, and not to be taken lightly! The Trustee is described as a "fiduciary" – someone who acts totally for the benefit of someone else – in this case, the beneficiaries of the trust. This is a very high standard and comes with liability if the Trustee fails to act properly. Trustees have several basic duties:

Duty to Administer Trusts

The Trustee must manage the trust according to its specific terms and for the period of time designated in the trust. The Trustee must consider both current and future beneficiaries when making management decisions. Trustees are expected to resign if they cannot meet these standards.

Duty of Loyalty

The Trustee must always act in the best interests of the beneficiaries, and must not place the Trustee's interests above those of the beneficiaries. Courts have imposed punitive damages when this duty is violated.

> Selecting a trustee is an extremely important decision.

Duty to Not Delegate Trustee Responsibilities

A Trustee is responsible to the trustmaker and the beneficiaries to personally carry out the management of the trust assets and follow the trust instructions. If the Trustee is a corporate entity, it should not delegate to one individual (such as a trust officer) the right to determine distributions. Rather, decisions should be made by a committee or board.

Duty to Keep and Render Accounts

The Trustee has the role of a record-keeper and provider of transactional details. The Trustee is responsible to provide accounting and notice to all beneficiaries, and is responsible for the accuracy of those records.

Duty to Furnish Information

In some cases, beneficiaries have the right to receive a copy of the trust – depending on the terms of the trust and state law. The Trustee must keep the beneficiaries informed of all facts necessary for them to protect their interests.

Duty to Exercise Reasonable Care and Skill

Trustees have the fiduciary duty to exercise reasonable care and skill in executing their duties and responsibilities. A professional Trustee is held to a higher standard of skill and care, and a higher standard of record-keeping than a non-professional (family) Trustee. The professional Trustee's actions are evaluated on their prudence, not on performance. Therefore, they tend to be more conservative with investments, and may earn lower returns.

CHAPTER 10   Duties of a Trustee

Duty to Take Control of Trust Property

The Trustee must ensure proper designation and titling of trust assets, and must keep trust assets separate from any other assets.

Duty of Impartiality

The Trustee must administer the trust so that each beneficiary is afforded the same level of benefits and protection. There can be no favoritism. This duty extends to current as well as future (successor) beneficiaries.

Duty with Respect to a Co-Trustee

Trustees hold dual accountability for their own actions and decisions, as well as the actions, inactions, or decisions of any Co-Trustee. While many Co-Trustees divide duties between them, it is important for all Trustees to continually monitor all Co-Trustees to ensure that everyone is acting properly in their fiduciary capacity.

CHAPTER 11

What Do I Do With My Stuff?

How to keep the kids from fighting over your personal property

It might come as a surprise to you, but more family battles are fought over Mom and Dad's personal property (the "stuff") than are fought over the money that is left behind. That may be because personal effects have worth to the kids beyond their intrinsic value. Personal property comes with memories, attachments, and sentimental value that are hard to quantify.

So how do you ensure that the kids won't fight over your stuff? The answer is to specifically include your personal property in your estate planning. Now, it would be impractical (if not impossible) to list every item of personal property that you own, designate where it goes after you're gone, and put it into your will or trust. It would probably be incomplete or out of date within days – and would require a complete update to your estate plan every month or so!

> Most family fights start over "stuff."

The right way to include personal property in your plan is through the use of a Quitclaim Bill of Sale and the Personal Property Memorandum. The Bill of Sale is a general document that transfers your existing personal property into your trust, thus giving your Trustee the authority to deal with it after your death.

CHAPTER 11 What Do I Do With My Stuff?

The Personal Property Memorandum is a specific list of items that are important to you or your loved ones, with instructions on who should receive those items when you're gone. You are unlikely to list every single item of personal property you own, but instead should focus on those things that are family heirlooms, antiques, collectibles, or of significant financial or sentimental value.

The Personal Property Memorandum can be updated whenever you desire. All you do is tear up the old one and fill out a new one, and your instructions are changed. No need to involve your attorney or advisors every time you change your mind about a recipient. (We had one client who on the first of every year, changed her distributions based on which children came to visit her during the previous year, and which ones didn't!)

One of the best ways to make these decisions is to talk to your children ahead of time, and find out which things they really value – and if they have specific preferences on what they receive. If more than one child wants the same item, that will give you time to figure out a fair system for distribution. We can provide several ideas on how you might accomplish that.

There are also many ways to determine distribution after death for those items that aren't specifically named – everything from having the children take turns picking things out – to an "auction" using Monopoly money – to having an estate sale and splitting the cash proceeds equally.

One other option you might consider is to give away some of your prized possessions while you are still alive and well – especially if you're not using them. That way you can have the pleasure of seeing your loved ones enjoying these possessions, and know that they won't be fighting over them after you're gone.

CHAPTER 12

Mental Disability Planning

Don't put your family through a guardianship proceeding

If a person becomes mentally disabled without proper planning in place, his or her affairs can only be managed by someone else when so ordered by a judge in a public forum called a guardianship hearing. In some states, it's referred to as a conservatorship. Some states differentiate between the two terms, using "guardian" to describe the person who is in charge of your person, and "conservator" to describe the person who is in charge of your money. Regardless of what it's called in your state, the process is costly (a recent case with which we're familiar cost nearly $30,000), and it's time-consuming.

And regardless of the rules in your state, this formal proceeding should be the last choice for transferring control of your affairs to someone you trust. With proper planning, it can be avoided altogether.

In a guardianship proceeding, it must first be established that you can no longer manage your financial affairs. Who will make that decision? The judge may appoint a doctor who doesn't know you personally, or may take the word of your attending physician but without a second medical opinion, and without consulting family members who know you best. In any case, the method of determination is out of your control.

Next, the judge will decide who will manage your affairs. Will he or she appoint a family member? How will that person be chosen? Will it be your spouse or a court-appointed guardian? Will it be one of your children, based on age or

CHAPTER 12   Mental Disability Planning

geographic proximity – regardless of their relationship with you, or their skill in money management? Again, the decision is out of your control.

One of the primary goals of virtually every client is to retain control throughout your lifetime, including any periods when you might be mentally disabled. With proper planning, that goal can be accomplished.

One of the best planning methods we've discovered for protecting you during disability, and avoiding court involvement in your affairs, is to establish within your revocable living trust instructions for a "disability panel" to determine when you are disabled, and name disability trustees who can manage your affairs when you cannot.

> All it takes to avoid a public court-ordered guardianship is to plan ahead.

The disability panel members will be chosen by YOU. You'll definitely want a medical opinion, but you don't have to limit it to that. For example, instead of leaving the decision to just any doctor, or even two doctors, you can be very specific. You might want to include your primary care physician, for example, along with a specialist who might be treating the specific cause of your disability.

On the other hand, it is often your family members who will know (better than the doctors) if you are having problems handling your day-to-day affairs. So your disability panel may also include one or more family members along with the doctors. The panel who determines your disability can also be given authority to decide that you have recovered from your disability, and then move your affairs back into your control.

Most importantly, in addition to deciding who will determine when you are disabled, the instructions will also include who you want to manage your affairs after disability is determined, and how your affairs are to be managed. You can leave instructions on a wide variety of topics including:

- what type of housing and medical care you desire
- how you want your assets to be invested

CHAPTER 12   Mental Disability Planning

- how to take care of minor dependents
- how to continue gifting programs you may have started
- and much more.

All it takes to avoid a public court-ordered guardianship is to plan ahead.

CHAPTER 13

Planning for IRAs, 401(k)s, and other Retirement Money

The IRA Inheritance Trust will protect it and let it grow tax-free

Background

For many of our clients, their IRA (whether traditional or Roth) is their most problematic asset. That's because without proper planning, these retirement accounts can be subject to triple taxation! They could be hit with federal estate taxes, federal income taxes, and state income taxes – resulting in a combined rate of over 65%! But the tax problem can be overcome with proper planning.

An Overview of the IRA Inheritance Trust™

Many people are familiar with the revocable living trust (RLT) that often serves as the foundation document of your estate plan. The IRA Inheritance Trust is also a revocable trust, but it is separate from your primary RLT. It is established specifically to be the beneficiary of your IRA or other retirement plan.

We find that when the IRA is directed to a separate trust at death, it alerts the beneficiaries and trustees that the IRA will receive special treatment. It ensures

CHAPTER 13   Planning for IRAs, 401(k)s, and other Retirement Money

that instructions specific to handling IRAs to avoid excess taxation are being followed. It's also easier for the custodian of the IRA to understand, accept, and properly administer a separate trust that deals only with the retirement plan, and not with all the other assets that you leave to your loved ones.

How Does it Work?

You, as owner of your IRA, will begin by setting up a trust that meets the technical requirements to be qualified by the IRS as a "stretch-out." The Trustees and distribution patterns of this trust will usually be the same as the primary living trust. For example, if you are dividing all of your assets equally between three children, the IRA Inheritance Trust will usually also be divided equally among the children. And – just like the primary living trust – the IRA trust can be amended to make changes as required.

When you go to sit on your cloud, the trust will ensure that the IRA account is properly re-titled. Any required minimum distributions (RMDs) will pour into the IRA trust. The trust instructions will then determine when the funds will be paid out and to whom. Those instructions will also determine how the distributions are taxed. The beneficiaries will often choose to receive those required minimum distributions, though some may have them held in trust for further tax-deferred growth.

The Benefits of the IRA Inheritance Trust

Ensure "Stretch-out"

With the tax law changes in 2003, the IRS allows the required minimum distributions (RMDs) of inherited IRAs to be calculated using the beneficiaries' life expectancy. This results in smaller distributions and longer tax-deferred compounded growth. Unfortunately, most inherited IRAs never get to enjoy this "stretch" because the IRA is mishandled. This mishandling happens either because the beneficiaries don't understand the rules or they just want to spend the money. The IRA Inheritance Trust allows you to "lock up" the IRA and ensure

CHAPTER 13 Planning for IRAs, 401(k)s, and other Retirement Money

the stretch-out while still allowing the beneficiary access to those funds should they be required in an emergency.

Divorce Protection

IRAs should not be included in a divorce decree. However, going through a divorce is a very stressful time and IRAs are frequently seen by divorce attorneys as an easily accessible pot of money to fund a marital dissolution agreement. The IRA Inheritance Trust will protect against a beneficiary losing the inherited IRA through a divorce.

Protection for Minors

People are apprehensive about leaving money to minors because they do not know how that person will turn out as an adult, and do not want to fund self-destructive habits. With the IRA Inheritance Trust you can name a trustee that ensures that the assets are there for the minors' benefit but will not be used to exacerbate any character flaws.

Lawsuit, Creditor, and Bankruptcy Protection

Inherited IRAs should be protected from the claims of creditors, including lawsuits and bankruptcy. However, when the money is withdrawn from the IRA, as most beneficiaries do, those funds are subject to the claims of creditors. With the IRA Inheritance Trust you can protect not only the principal of the IRA but also the required minimum distributions.

Protection from Losing Government Benefits

For those individuals who receive government benefits, such as heirs with special needs, any asset left in an inheritance can be subject to the pay-back rules. With the IRA Inheritance Trust you can be certain that those monies will be used to give that beneficiary the "extras" in life and not be used to pay back Uncle Sam.

Minimize Future Estate Taxes

If IRA assets are left to a beneficiary in his or her individual name they may be subject to estate taxes when the beneficiary passes away, because the inherited

CHAPTER 13   Planning for IRAs, 401(k)s, and other Retirement Money

IRA is includable in the beneficiary's estate. However, if the IRA is left in the IRA Inheritance Trust, it will never be estate taxable again.

> "If you and your spouse have more than $300,000 in IRAs, 401(k)s or 403(b)s, or other retirement plans, the IRA Inheritance Trust is a MUST!"

Leave a Legacy in Your Name

Eventually we are all going to pass on to our greater glory. It is how we are remembered by those who knew and loved us that keeps us alive forever. With the IRA Inheritance Trust, a check will be coming to your beneficiaries with your name on it for their benefit every quarter. This will be part of your legacy.

Like any other planning tool, the IRA Inheritance Trust must be carefully coordinated with all your other planning documents and strategies.

CHAPTER 13 Planning for IRAs, 401(k)s, and other Retirement Money

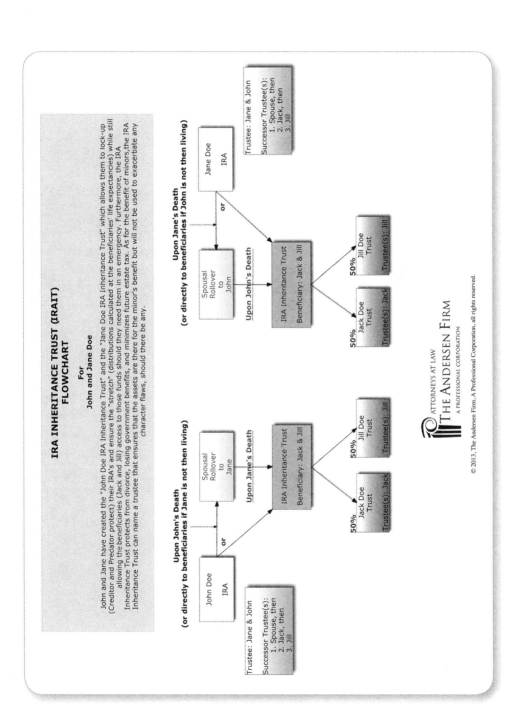

CHAPTER 14

Federal and State Estate Taxes

Quantifying the taxes, hoping for the best, but planning for the worst

Recent tax law changes have brought a certain degree of "certainty" to the subject of estate taxes and related transfer taxes. However, history teaches us that this area of the law is never truly and permanently "settled." Many of our clients have been asking if they should just wait to plan for federal and state estate taxes until the law gets "settled." Our answer is a resounding "NO!" You should not wait for two reasons:

- Tax laws are never settled. They change almost annually.

- Life is uncertain – if you knew for sure the day you would pass away, you could postpone your planning until the day before, but most of us don't have that knowledge.

> Estate and Gift Tax laws are never settled. Hope for the best, and plan for the worst.

So we recommend that all our clients plan according to current laws, but build in flexibility that can adapt to changes in those laws. Of course, we also recommend that our clients review their plans on a regular basis, and update the details of the plan as required from time to time.

CHAPTER 14   Federal and State Estate Taxes

At any given time, by knowing the total value of your assets, we are able to determine whether or not you have an estate tax problem, and we can calculate with some specificity what your taxes would be on both the federal and state levels if you passed away today.

Then we can implement one or more tax-focused planning strategies (such as those described in Part Two of this book) to reduce or eliminate those taxes. Instead of using specific numbers that are tied to today's laws, we design our plans using general methods of measurement that will flex and adapt regardless of the specific numbers in effect at the time of your death.

CHAPTER 15

How Do I Calculate My Federal and Local Estate Tax

Just call us and we'll tell you the current temperature and today's forecast – if you don't like the weather, just wait and it may get better (or worse)

There is a lot of confusion when it comes to estate taxes - and that's not surprising since things change so often. Some people even think that estate taxes no longer exist! But estate taxes are like the weather – the sun that shines brightly today may be invisible tomorrow. And the clear skies that you now enjoy may be filled with snow next week. That's why we've become estate planning "storm chasers" – so that we can keep up with the weather and issue warnings and bulletins to our clients when needed.

It's true that the federal estate tax was actually temporarily repealed for the year 2010. However, following tax law signed into place during December of 2010, the federal estate tax

> In the last forty years, estate tax rules have been changed significantly at least 12 times. Most times it was reinstated to help pay for huge deficits associated with the cost of various wars.

CHAPTER 15   How Do I Calculate My Federal and Local Estate Tax

came back retroactive to January 1, 2010. Historically, the estate tax has come and gone several times. It was first enacted in the late 1700s only to be repealed 4 years later in 1801. The estate tax was reinstated in 1862 to provide funds during the Civil War and was repealed 8 years later in 1870. It came back again for four years between 1898 and 1902.

The modern version of the estate tax was enacted in 1916 and modified many times over the years. In the last forty years, estate tax rules have been changed significantly at least twelve times. Most times it was reinstated to help pay for huge deficits associated with the cost of various wars. Therefore, based on historical precedent and current deficits, you should probably expect the estate tax to be with us in some form for a long time.

In 2011, the reappearing tax law gave each person an exemption from estate taxes of $5 million ($10 million for a married couple with proper planning), with a 35% tax on any assets exceeding those amounts. However, as that law expired at the end of 2012, the American Taxpayer Relief Act (ATRA) of 2012 raised the exemption to $5.25 million per person for 2013 (indexed for inflation in subsequent years), with a 40% tax on any assets exceeding these amounts. More changes may be afoot under the President's proposed 2014 budget, including potentially lowering the exemption to $3.5 million per person, with a 45% tax on any assets exceeding these amounts.

The point is that the future of the estate tax at any time is uncertain. We can never predict with certainty what will happen next. Like the TV weatherman, we can make some educated guesses about the future, but we can't always be exact in our predictions. That's why it's important to check with a professional whenever you need to know the current estate tax "weather conditions" and "forecast."

CHAPTER 16

Estate and Income Tax Planning

You only have 6 choices, and one of them is to pay the tax

1. Pay the Tax This is the option that Uncle Sam wants you to choose and is the default option if you don't choose any of the other five options. Upon the second spouse's death any amount over and above the federal exemption amount will be taxed. This also is true for any amount over and above the state exemption amounts depending on the state where you officially reside.

2. Spend it All Spending down the estate by taking long vacations, buying more expensive cars, and eating out at fancy restaurants, is a way to avoid paying the estate tax. However, this option does not appeal to many people who have worked their entire lives to obtain the wealth they have – and want to make sure it will last for the remainder of their lives and on to the next generation.

3. Gift it to Charity Gifting any amounts over the current exemption amount to a charity or charities will negate any federal estate tax. For most families, charity starts at home and we would rather see those monies go to our children and beneficiaries.

> You only have six choices – and one of them is to pay the tax.

4. Gift it to Beneficiaries A gifting program properly implemented and adhered to is a great way to pass wealth down to beneficiaries and out of the estate. However, the gifting program must have enough time to make an impact and will not be effective if it is started late in life.

5. Advanced Planning Techniques There are over 60 different estate planning techniques that can zero out estate taxes no matter how large the estate. Several of these techniques are discussed in the following chapters.

6. Irrevocable Life Insurance Trust The irrevocable life insurance trust or ILIT is a special type of trust that holds and is the beneficiary of, a special type of insurance. The insurance inside this trust is guaranteed level premium, guaranteed benefit, and can be placed on the life of one spouse or both spouses. The payout from the policy is not estate taxable and is specifically earmarked to pay the estate taxes. This option is one of the simplest and most efficient ways to deal with the estate tax.

CHAPTER 17

Where You Live Matters

Avoid state inheritance and estate taxes, and win a second home

In addition to the federal estate tax, some states impose their own tax on a deceased person's property. Some states use an "inheritance" tax, while others use an "estate" tax.

An inheritance tax is based on who receives a deceased person's property and how the beneficiary is related to the deceased person. The exemption amount and tax rate depend on who inherits the property. In all of the states that collect an inheritance tax, spouses are completely exempt from the tax, while in some states children and grandchildren are also completely exempt. In other states children and grandchildren are separated into one class of beneficiaries and other close relatives (such as brothers and sisters or nieces and nephews) are grouped into a different class. Each class will then receive an exemption from the tax as well as pay a specific tax rate. The 6 states that currently impose an inheritance tax include: Iowa, Kentucky, Maryland, Nebraska, New Jersey and Pennsylvania.

An estate tax levied by a state is based on the value of the deceased person's estate and not on who gets what. Even if your estate isn't big enough to owe federal estate tax, your state may still tax you. In addition, if you are a resident of a state that does not impose an estate tax but you own real estate in a state that does, then your estate may owe an estate tax in the state where the real estate is located. The tax rate is usually quite a bit less than the federal estate tax rates. Property left to a surviving spouse

CHAPTER 17 Where You Live Matters

> *Avoid state inheritance and estate taxes, and win a second home!*

is usually exempt from state estate tax, just as it is exempt from federal estate tax. The 16 states that currently impose an estate tax are: Connecticut, Delaware, District of Columbia, Hawaii, Illinois, Maine, Maryland, Massachusetts, Minnesota, New Jersey, New York, Oregon, Rhode Island, Tennessee, Vermont, and Washington. As of the date of publication, Delaware's estate tax is only supposed to be in effect for deaths occurring on or before June 30, 2013.

Note that while the Tennessee statutes refer to its state death tax as an "inheritance tax," the tax is based on the overall value of the deceased person's estate, not on who gets what. Therefore, we have categorized Tennessee's death tax as an "estate tax," though some may differ. In any event, under current Tennessee law, this death tax in Tennessee will be completely phased out effective January 1, 2016.

Remember that simply owning real estate in one of these states can be enough to trigger the tax – at least on those assets within the state. We can advise you on what you might face in your specific situation, and what options you have to avoid additional taxation.

Many of our clients decide to establish residency in a state that does not levy any taxes after death. In some cases, if you own a home in that state, register to vote there, and have a driver's license from that state, that is probably sufficient to establish that state as your residence. Other states are extraordinarily aggressive about exerting their tax schemes on anyone who has any contact with the state.

Even if you feel that you can't afford to buy a second home in one of these states, when you calculate what you'll save in state inheritance or estate taxes, you may find that your savings will cover the cost of that second home.

CHAPTER 18

Insurance and the Irrevocable Life Insurance Trust (ILIT)

Using insurance to pay part or all of the estate, inheritance, and income tax, while keeping the value of the insurance out of your estate

We believe that any comprehensive estate planning session will include a discussion of life insurance. Most people think about life insurance as a source of funds to replace lost income after the death of a breadwinner, or to provide liquidity for immediate expenses and taxes after someone passes away. Those are important uses that every planner will consider.

However, life insurance is a tool that can be used effectively throughout the entire planning process for a wide variety of purposes, including to leverage or reposition assets for estate planning and transfer purposes.

The problem, however, is that the death proceeds of any insurance policy owned by you, will be taxed in your estate. This is where the Irrevocable Life Insurance Trust (ILIT) comes into play because the IRS cannot assess estate taxes against an asset that is not owned by your estate, and in which you have no "incidents of ownership" when you pass away.

CHAPTER 15   Insurance and the Irrevocable Life Insurance Trust (ILIT)

If your insurance policy is owned by an ILIT instead of by you personally, the proceeds will not be taxed. However, there is a risk in merely transferring ownership of an existing insurance policy from your own name into an ILIT. The IRS has a three-year "look back" period, and will argue that any transfers of ownership in the three years prior to your death may still be counted as part of the estate for tax purposes. That's why most clients will set up an ILIT and then have the ILIT purchase a new insurance policy, so that the client will have no incidents of ownership.

> An ILIT can greatly increase the value of the life insurance proceeds your beneficiaries will receive.

The ILIT Process

When using an ILIT as part of your estate plan, it's important that the following steps be carefully followed in order. To do otherwise is to risk the insurance proceeds being pulled back into your estate:

1. The ILIT is drafted by your estate planning attorney to incorporate all your wishes.

2. You (as the insured person) sign the ILIT as the Trustmaker, and it will also be signed by your appointed Trustee.

3. The Trustee obtains a tax ID number and opens a bank account in the name of the ILIT.

4. You make a gift of the initial insurance premium to the ILIT, which the Trustee deposits into the trust's bank account.

5. The Trustee prepares "Crummey" notices which inform the beneficiaries of their limited right to withdraw their share of the gift from the ILIT. (The name for these notices is not a comment on their quality, but rather based on the name of a court case.)

CHAPTER 15   Insurance and the Irrevocable Life Insurance Trust (ILIT)

6. The beneficiaries sign an acknowledgment that they received the Crummey notice, and return that acknowledgement to the Trustee.

7. The beneficiaries allow their limited withdrawal rights to lapse. (The period of time it takes for the rights to elapse is specified in the trust.)

8. Once the rights have elapsed, the Trustee uses the money in the trust to pay the insurance premium, and the policy is issued showing the ILIT as both the owner and beneficiary of the trust.

9. Each time an insurance premium comes due (usually annually) steps 5-9 are repeated.

Things to Consider When Designing an ILIT

There are several things to be considered when designing an ILIT.

The first is who will serve as the Trustee of the trust. You cannot serve as your own Trustee, because that would be an "incident of ownership" which would cause the insurance proceeds to be included in your estate. You could choose your spouse, a child, or some other relative to serve as Trustee, but the person selected must be responsible enough to handle all the required duties listed above (including ensuring that Crummey notices are sent in a timely manner and premiums are properly paid).

The second consideration is how the beneficiaries will receive the proceeds. For example, a trust can be established for the benefit of the surviving spouse, children, or other beneficiaries, thereby removing the proceeds from the spouse's or children's estates, as well as protecting the insurance proceeds from creditors, judgments, or future divorces.

The third consideration is who will be entitled to the Crummey withdrawal rights. The larger the group of beneficiaries, the more the annual premium can be covered with gifts, without exceeding the annual gift tax exclusion. A larger premium will result in a larger death benefit. So some clients may want to include children and grandchildren to maximize the number of beneficiaries.

However, every beneficiary must receive a Crummey notice (although the notice to a minor will actually go to their parent or guardian). Each beneficiary of the trust with a withdrawal right must have a fully vested share of the trust, which may or may not be your intent. Also keep in mind that each person with a withdrawal right will have their share of the ILIT included in their own estate upon their death.

Additional Considerations When Using an ILIT

An ILIT is not without its challenges. For one thing, it is irrevocable. That means that once it is established, it cannot be changed. Because the ILIT will be the owner of the life insurance policy, you will have no control over it. You will not be able to make loans or withdrawals of the cash value, and you can't change the beneficiaries. The Trustee will be in control.

Also, the formalities and order of the process described earlier must be carefully followed each year, or gift taxes may be triggered.

Conclusion

An ILIT can greatly increase the value of the life insurance proceeds your beneficiaries will receive, because they will not be subject to estate taxes upon your death. And while you may assume that you won't have to worry about estate taxes, please keep a few things in mind:

- The laws and exemption amounts change constantly.

- Your eventual net worth is not always predictable.

- If you own your insurance policies personally, they are included in your estate for tax purposes. If the policies are large enough, those insurance proceeds alone may make you subject to estate taxes!

CHAPTER 18   Insurance and the Irrevocable Life Insurance Trust (ILIT)

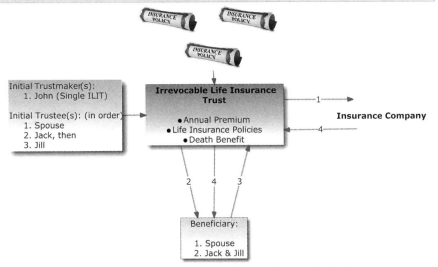

CHAPTER 19

Buying Insurance

*Use an advisor who is a
knowledgeable insurance professional, not a salesman*

Many advisors use life and long term care insurance as tools in an estate plan. Life insurance may be used for income replacement at the death or disability of a breadwinner, as a way to create an inheritance, to replace assets that are given to charity, or to pay estate taxes. Long term care insurance is used to offset the high costs of medical care during long illnesses that can lead to wealth erosion.

With the many choices of insurance plans available, an insurance professional is necessary to make sure you obtain the most appropriate coverage based on your personalized needs and purposes. There is a difference between an insurance professional and an insurance salesman. As in any industry, the quality of advice you receive can vary greatly from one practitioner to the next.

In our experience, there are many insurance salesmen who are motivated, both in their advice and the choice of insurance companies, by the commission they will receive. An insurance professional, on the other hand, will work closely with a client's other professional advisors, focusing only on the needs of the client, and doing whatever is in the client's best interest.

CHAPTER 19   Buying Insurance

How Can I Tell The Difference?

When you need an insurance professional to be involved in your estate planning, the best way to find one may be through the recommendation of your financial advisor, CPA, or estate planning attorney. These experienced professionals will have had many opportunities to work with insurance professionals, and will usually know the ones that are the best fit for your situation.

If you prefer to find your own professional, here are some questions that might be helpful in determining who is a professional, and who is merely a salesman:

1. How much experience do you have in the use of insurance for estate and financial planning?

2. Have you ever worked with a team of advisors before?

3. What is your typical case and client profile?

4. Are you captive to one insurance company or can you represent several?

5. If several, what percentage of your business is given to each of the companies you recommend?

6. What are the industry ratings of the companies you are recommending?

7. How do you get compensated?

8. Do you have a CLU or ChFC designation? (There are some great insurance professionals that do not have a Certified Life Underwriter (CLU) or Chartered Financial Consultant (ChFC) designation. The lack of a designation should not automatically disqualify an insurance practitioner, but having a designation such as these shows an extra level of dedication to learning and growth, and can often be a good indicator.)

CHAPTER 19   Buying Insurance

Insurance Agents, Insurance Brokers, and Insurance Companies

An insurance company is the entity that collects your premium and contractually agrees to pay out a benefit in the event of death, disability, long-term care needs, or other events. While there may be 600 or more insurance companies in existence at any time, most insurance professionals tend to recommend from among the top 30 or so.

You want to be sure the agent is making recommendations that are not based exclusively on the commission the agent will earn. If you are getting recommendations to use a company you've never heard of (Night Life of Cuba, for example) you'll want to proceed with caution – and be sure to check out the official ratings of the company. There are several companies that rate the quality of insurance companies based on financial strength, longevity, paying claims, and the likelihood that they'll be around to pay the insurance proceeds when needed. Rating companies include A.M. Best, Moody's, Weiss, Duff & Phelps, and Standard & Poor's.

An insurance agent is typically a representative of the insurance company. Agents must be licensed in the states in which they do business and licensed with the various companies they represent. "Captive" agents typically do the vast majority of their insurance business with one company and may be contractually prohibited from selling other companies' products. Some agents can be licensed with multiple carriers and make products from all of those companies available to their clients.

> Use an advisor who is a knowledgeable insurance professional, not merely a salesman.

Insurance brokers differ in that they more often represent the client than an insurance company. Brokers typically have additional tests they must pass as well as bonding requirements that may be determined by the state in which they are licensed. Most often a broker will represent many companies and offer multiple alternatives to their clients. There are a wide array

CHAPTER 19 Buying Insurance

of choices, prices, products, and financial strength of companies, which should all be taken into account during the insurance acquisition process. Generally, the more options you have, the better.

PART TWO

Advanced Planning

CHAPTER 20

Advanced Planning Techniques

*When you don't want to give it to the government
and insurance is not the (total) answer*

Estate planning includes a wide variety of sophisticated strategies and tools, especially designed for those clients who face exorbitant estate tax liabilities. Often the fastest and easiest solution to the tax problem is purchasing enough insurance to cover the taxes, and keeping those proceeds out of the estate in an Irrevocable Life Insurance Trust as described in Chapter 18.

Unfortunately, not everyone can get life insurance. Because of age or health problems, some of our clients are simply uninsurable. Others may not have the cash flow to add new insurance premiums, and some clients just don't like insurance for one reason or another. That's when other advanced planning techniques become very important. Some of these strategies can even be combined with insurance for additional effectiveness.

In the following chapters you'll learn the basics of how these techniques can work to keep your hard-earned wealth in the family, or direct it to causes you care about, rather than having it go to the IRS.

You'll see a whole "alphabet soup" of acronyms – legal shorthand that makes the techniques easier to discuss. Don't let all the strange names intimidate you – they are all just different approaches to saving taxes.

CHAPTER 20   Advanced Planning Techniques

Note that most of these strategies involve the use of irrevocable trusts – trusts that for the most part cannot be changed. They are not to be entered into lightly. Only you and your professional advisors can determine if any of these strategies are the right solutions to your estate planning challenges, and which ones will best serve to meet your goals.

CHAPTER 21

The Grantor Deemed Owner Trust (GDOT)

How to buy insurance and not incur gift taxes

What is a GDOT?

A Grantor Deemed Owner Trust (GDOT) is an irrevocable trust that is treated differently for federal income tax purposes than for federal estate tax purposes. For estate tax purposes, any gifts you make to the GDOT will be treated as a completed gift, meaning the gifts are excluded from your taxable estate (just like with the ILIT). However, for income tax purposes, you are treated as the owner of the GDOT assets. As a result, you are responsible for the income taxes.

Paying the income taxes on assets that you gift to the GDOT is the equivalent of making additional tax-free gifts to the beneficiaries of the GDOT. This is because the GDOT funds will not be depleted by payment of income taxes generated by the income of the GDOT. As a result, the beneficiaries will receive more assets in trust than if the GDOT was required to pay its own income taxes. This additional gift does not count against your lifetime gift tax exemption or the annual exclusion for gift tax.

A common planning technique is to couple a GDOT to an intermediate business entity such as a Limited Liability Company (LLC) that serves one or more valid objectives and business purposes. Valid objectives can include gift and estate tax planning, asset protection planning, business preservation planning, or to

CHAPTER 21   The Grantor Deemed Owner Trust (GDOT)

facilitate an annual gifting program. Valid business purposes might include business succession planning, continuity of management, to facilitate intra-family loans, or to plan and protect a family's future.

How it Works

These are the typical steps you would follow:

- You establish an LLC.

- You make a gift of cash or property to the LLC and take back LLC membership interests (often set up as 1% voting, and 99% non-voting interests).

- You establish the GDOT and name a Trustee other than yourself or a beneficiary of the GDOT.

- Next, you SELL the 99% LLC non-voting interests to the trustee of the GDOT in return for a promissory note.

- The note must bear an adequate rate of interest. Sometimes the note requires the payment of annual interest with a balloon payment of principal at a later point in time.

- Your LLC interests that are sold to the GDOT should include income-producing assets that are expected to appreciate in value. That way, the GDOT will have sufficient funds so that the Trustee can use the income produced by the GDOT assets to make the promissory note payments to you.

> How to buy insurance and not incur gift taxes.

Advantages of the GDOT

For income tax purposes, there is no tax on the transfer from you to your own LLC. Furthermore, the subsequent sale of LLC interests to the GDOT is not recognized (since you are treated as the owner of the GDOT assets for income tax purposes) and there will be no taxable gain on the sale, thus avoiding income or capital gains tax. However, for estate tax purposes, any assets sold to the GDOT would be excluded from your estate.

Your estate will own the promissory note and receive periodic payments of interest and principal as provided in the note. Although the promissory note is included in your taxable estate at your death, the value of the note is fixed at the time of the sale. Therefore, if the assets sold to the GDOT appreciate in value from the time of sale to your date of death, the appreciation is excluded from your taxable estate. The assets of the GDOT, including all of the appreciation, will pass estate tax free to the GDOT's beneficiaries, according to the GDOT's terms.

The GDOT and Insurance

The GDOT is especially advantageous when the internal cash flow is enough to cover not only the promissory note payments to you, but also to pay the premiums for one or more life insurance policies.

You learned in Chapter 18 that when you use a traditional Irrevocable Life Insurance Trust (ILIT) to own your insurance, it works to keep the death proceeds out of your taxable estate. However, the ILIT structure also requires annual gifts, annual Crummey Notices to all beneficiaries, and an annual filing of a federal Form 709 gift tax return. If instead, the GDOT is buying the insurance from the cash flow of the LLC assets, there is no annual gifting, no notices to be sent to beneficiaries, and no gift tax returns.

Things to Consider When Using a GDOT

Like most advanced tax planning strategies, the GDOT also comes with some planning realities to consider. For one thing, it is an irrevocable transaction. You therefore lose use of the assets, and give away the potential upside future growth. It can create "phantom income" – income you don't actually receive, but upon which you are taxed. Finally, it requires a detailed cash analysis, and should be entered into only upon careful consideration and advice from your professional advisory team.

CHAPTER 21 The Grantor Deemed Owner Trust (GDOT)

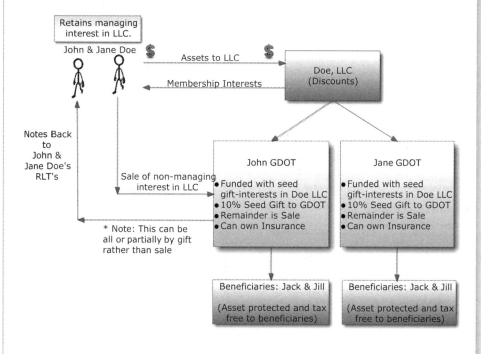

CHAPTER 22

Buildup Equity Retirement Trusts (BERTs)

A gift for your spouse – protecting the asset, removing the value from your estate, and providing for your beneficiaries

The trust we affectionately call "BERT" is a tax-sheltered trust for the benefit of your spouse. It has the following advantages:

- Assets are exempt from gift tax

- Assets are exempt from estate tax

- Assets are protected from creditors and predators

- It creates a "nest egg" for each spouse over which he or she has control

- Upon a spouse's death, the assets pass tax-free

How it Works

Most estate planners use the unlimited marital deduction for gifts to a spouse, and the annual gift tax exclusion for gifts to children or other beneficiaries.

CHAPTER 22   Buildup Equity Retirement Trusts (BERTs)

Instead, with a BERT, the "donor" spouse creates an irrevocable trust for the benefit of the "donee" spouse for his or her life, with the remainder passing to the beneficiaries upon the donee spouse's death.

Next, the donor makes gifts to the trust under the annual exclusion rules, in an amount not to exceed $5,000 or 5% of the value of the trust assets, whichever is greater. Of course, the gift also cannot exceed the maximum annual gift exclusion amount.

The donee spouse is the Trustee of the trust, and can use the assets at any time to provide for his or her health, maintenance, and education; yet the assets remain protected from creditors and predators.

Case Study

For example, let's assume that each spouse forms a BERT for the benefit of the other spouse, and makes a gift every year for the next 30 years of the maximum allowable under the current gift tax exclusion limits for each year.

Assuming annual gifts of $5,000 and a growth rate of 8%, in 30 years the BERTs will each be worth approximately $1,500,000. These funds are protected, but each spouse can access their own BERT for health, maintenance, and education – in other words, to meet that spouse's needs.

By making modest gifts into the BERTs each year, the clients create an additional reserve of cash that is not subject to estate taxes, above and beyond the estate tax exemption allowed by current law. It won't matter if the estate tax exemption is at $5 million, $3.5 million, $1 million, or whatever Congress decides to do with the tax laws in the future.

Income Tax Treatment of the BERT

As described in the previous chapter, a BERT can be structured as a grantor trust, which means the donor spouse, who has created the trust, pays the trust income tax. If the BERTs are structured as grantor trusts, the trust assets grow without being reduced by taxes. As an added benefit, payment of the income tax by the donor spouse further reduces the size of his or her estate.

The BERT is Flexible

An annual gifting program using BERTs can be very flexible:

- Gifts can be as simple as cash, or as complex as closely-held business interests which qualify for valuation discounts.

- Gifts can be made annually, or only as frequently as the donor spouse chooses.

- Terms of the trust can specify that benefits to the donee spouse will end upon divorce, remarriage, or any other event defined by the donor spouse.

Supercharged BERTs

The power of the BERT is found in the power of compounding tax-free interest and growth over many years. Even though the BERT is a powerful tool using modest annual exclusion gifts, there is a way to "supercharge" the benefits by starting with a bigger initial gift.

> A gift for your spouse – protecting the asset, removing the value from your estate, and providing for your beneficiaries

Suppose that each spouse gifts $250,000 the first year, using up part of his or her lifetime tax exclusion. Each year thereafter, each spouse gifts that year's maximum gift allowed under gift tax exclusion rules. Assuming annual gifts of $5,000 and a growth rate of 8%, each BERT could be worth approximately $2,500,000 in 20 years, and $6,500,000 after 30 years!

The most powerful use of this tool is for each spouse to give discounted interests in the amount of the lifetime gift tax exclusion. Obviously, because of the magic

CHAPTER 22 Buildup Equity Retirement Trusts (BERTs)

of compounding interest, the sooner you establish the BERT trust and start your gifting program, the better the result.

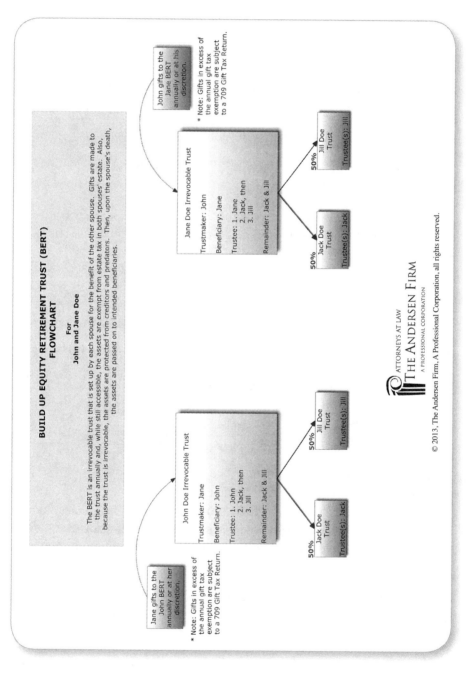

CHAPTER 23

Qualified Personal Residence Trusts (QPRTs)

Remove the value of your home from your estate, protect it, and live in it just as you do now

A Qualified Personal Residence Trust (QPRT) is an irrevocable trust that is designed to hold your primary and/or secondary residence.

How it Works

The QPRT is rather straightforward and easy to understand. Here are the basics:

1. Ownership of your residence is transferred by you into the QPRT.

2. For a period of years, called the "retained income period," you retain the right to use the residence.

3. At the end of the retained income period, the residence will pass to your heirs at a reduced value.

4. If you want to continue to live in the residence after the retained income period ends, you can rent it back from the heirs at fair market rent. That will allow you to transfer additional cash to

CHAPTER 23   Qualified Personal Residence Trusts (QPRTs)

your heirs and reduce your estate size, without using up any more of your estate tax exemption.

5. Assuming you survive the retained income period, the entire value of the residence, including any appreciation from the time you transferred it into the QPRT, will pass to your heirs outside of your estate, thus avoiding estate taxes.

6. Unfortunately, if you die before the retained income period ends, the entire benefit of the transaction would be lost because the residence would still be included in your estate. It would be valued at the fair market value at the time of your death.

7. By the same token, even if you die before the QPRT ends, your estate will be no worse off than if you had decided not to establish the QPRT.

What about Gift Taxes?

The transfer of the residence into the QPRT is considered a gift to the heirs for federal gift tax purposes. However, the gift will not be valued at the full fair market value of the residence at the time of transfer. Instead, it will be reduced by the value of your retained interest (the right to continue living in it).

> Remove the value of your home from your estate, protect it, and live in it just as you do now.

Both the retained interest and reversion values are calculated using actuarial tables established by the IRS, and vary upon the length of the retained income period chosen, interest rates on the date of transfer, and your age. Basically, the formula becomes: Fair Market Value of the Home (minus) the value of the Right to Live in the Home (equals) the Taxable Gift.

For example, if you are 65 years old and transfer your vacation home valued at $1 million into a 10-year QPRT, depending on the current interest rates, the gift may be valued at only $500,000 instead of $1 million. The longer the retained income period is, the lower the value of the gift. So a 15-year QPRT might bring the value of the gift down to $300,000 and a 20-year QPRT may reduce the value to $150,000.

One Income Tax Consideration

If the QPRT is used successfully (because you outlived the retained income period), the residence is not included at your estate at death. That is good from an estate tax perspective. However, one must think through the income tax picture when using a QPRT.

Assets that are included in your estate receive a "step-up" in cost basis at your death, avoiding capital gains tax on those assets that are liquidated by your heirs after inheritance. However, because the residence will not be part of the estate, it will not receive that step-up in basis. Instead, your heirs will receive the same cost basis you had in the residence. Therefore, if they decide to sell the home after your death, they will pay more in capital gains tax – thus offsetting some of the estate tax benefits of the QPRT.

For that reason, the QPRT is ideal for a residence that you know your heirs will likely retain in your family for many years to come. For example, a vacation home that the children have enjoyed throughout their lifetime is probably going to be kept, as well as a home that has been in the family for several generations.

CHAPTER 23 Qualified Personal Residence Trusts (QPRTs)

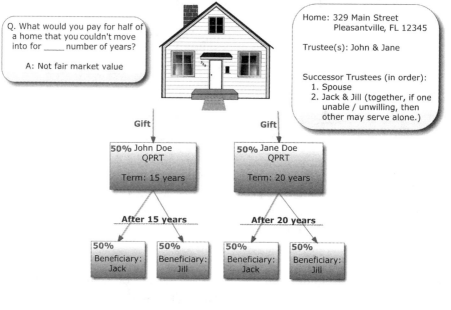

CHAPTER 24

Uniform Trust to Minors Accounts (UTMAs)

A word to the wise – do not use them

Many clients want to make gifts to minor grandchildren or great-grandchildren to help with future educational expenses or other needs. Outright gifts to minors are rare, however, because of the minor's lack of experience in making sound financial decisions. Instead, a common planning technique is to set up a minor's trust.

An alternative that some of our clients ask about is making a gift under the Uniform Transfers to Minors Act (formerly known as the Uniform Gifts to Minors Act). The UTMA (or UGMA) has been enacted in some form by every state and allows an adult custodian to invest the funds, and use them as needed for the minor's support and education.

The attraction of a UTMA gift is that it is usually simpler and less expensive because it involves opening an investment account rather than preparing a trust, and does not require a separate tax return. Instead the income is reported on the minor's individual income tax return, and minors tend to be in lower tax brackets.

CHAPTER 24   Uniform Trust to Minors Accounts (UTMAs)

However, UTMA gifts also have some major disadvantages:

- The biggest disadvantage is that once the child attains 21 years of age (and as young as 18 in some states), that child has the absolute right to control these assets - and do with them as he or she pleases. It doesn't matter if you said the funds were for college or to buy a first home – the child can spend them in any way, at any speed, and for anything they can imagine. You have completely lost control of the gift!

- There can only be one custodian of the UTMA funds and it can't be the donor without having those funds included in the donor's taxable estate for estate tax purposes. A trust, on the other hand, can have multiple trustees.

- The UTMA account is considered an asset for the minor. Depending on its size, it can negatively impact the child's eligibility for financial aid for higher education.

> A word to the wise about Uniform Trust to Minors Accounts (UTMAs) – DO NOT USE THEM

Because of these disadvantages, we recommend that our clients not use UTMA accounts to help their grandchildren and other heirs. By using a trust instead, you maintain maximum control to ensure that the funds are used for the good purposes you designate – helping rather than hurting the child in the long run.

If you are a grandparent, you might consider setting up a Legacy Trust (described in the next chapter) for your grandchild with the parent serving as the Trustee until the child reaches a certain age – maybe 35!

CHAPTER 24   Uniform Trust to Minors Accounts (UTMAs)

A Sobering Example

Consider the client who had set up an UTMA account for their grandchild. They were encouraged several times to stop contributing to the UTMA, and instead set up a trust for the minor's benefit. They kept saying that they were "thinking about it," but in the mean time, they kept contributing to the UTMA.

When the clients were killed in a car accident, the UTMA had grown to over $100,000. As soon as the grandchild reached legal age, he promptly bought two Harley Davidson motorcycles – one for himself and one for his girlfriend. They spent the next two years running around the country until the funds were exhausted.

CHAPTER 25

Legacy Trusts

Gifting to the children, grandchildren, and others while providing asset protection and maintaining some control (if you want to)

The Problem

Some parents and grandparents, who establish gifting programs for children and grandchildren, gift their assets outright to their beneficiaries. It's not uncommon to simply write a check each year to each of the beneficiaries to reduce the size of the giver's estate. Others use UTMA accounts as described in the previous chapter. Either method subjects those gifted assets to the creditors, predators, and divorcing spouses of those beneficiaries – in one case immediately, in the second case when they become of age according to state law.

There are a couple of problems with outright gifts at any age. The first problem is that studies have shown that when beneficiaries receive a gift or inheritance outright, it is gone within 18 months on average – regardless of the age of the beneficiary, and regardless of the size of that gift or inheritance!

The second problem is that even if the children don't spend the money, the check they receive is deposited into an account which is titled in the child's or grandchild's own name. That makes the gift subject to being taken in a lawsuit, business failure, divorce, or other of life's crises.

CHAPTER 25   Legacy Trusts

> *Gifting to the children, grandchildren, and others while providing asset protection and maintaining control.*

The Solution

The solution to this problem is a Legacy Trust. The Legacy Trust is an irrevocable trust that is set up by parents or grandparents specifically to be used for gifting to children or grandchildren. Because it's an irrevocable trust, the assets that are transferred to the Legacy Trust (and all future appreciation in the value of those assets) are removed from your estate and reduce your estate taxes.

If the trust is for a grandchild, for example, you can name his or her parents as Trustees and maintain control of how the assets are eventually used, and how and when they can be distributed. And as long as they remain inside the trust, they are protected from all creditors and predators – whether yours, the parent trustees, or the grandchildren themselves.

CHAPTER 25 Legacy Trusts

LEGACY TRUSTS (LT) FLOWCHART

For John and Jane Doe

John and Jane have created "Legacy Trusts" or gifting trusts for their children. This is designed for John and Jane to gift up to $14,000 per year (for 2013, indexed for inflation) into the Legacy Trusts (or more, provided they file a 709 gift tax return). Assets are then (1) out of John and Jane's taxable estate, (b) available to each beneficiary for health, education, and maintenance, (c) creditor & predator for the trust beneficiaries, and (d) under the control of the trustees.

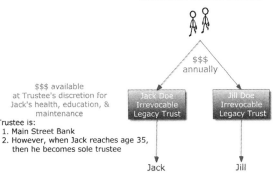

$$$ available at Trustee's discretion for Jack's health, education, & maintenance
- Trustee is:
  1. Main Street Bank
  2. However, when Jack reaches age 35, then he becomes sole trustee

$$$ available at Trustee's discretion for Jill's health, education, & maintenance
- Trustee is:
  1. Main Street Bank
  2. However, when Jill reaches age 35, then she becomes sole trustee

ATTORNEYS AT LAW
THE ANDERSEN FIRM
A PROFESSIONAL CORPORATION

© 2013, The Andersen Firm, A Professional Corporation, all rights reserved.

CHAPTER 26

Grantor Retained Annuity Trusts (GRATs)

*One way to gift appreciating assets to the kids (or others) –
but do it sooner rather than later*

Overview of the GRAT

A Grantor Retained Annuity Trust (GRAT) is an irrevocable trust to which the grantor transfers assets, while retaining the right to annual payments of a fixed amount of principal and interest for a prescribed number of years. At the end of the period, the remaining assets pass to the beneficiaries in accordance with the grantor's intentions.

The GRAT is typically used when you have an asset that you expect to appreciate significantly, and which you will want to eventually pass on to the beneficiaries. The IRS values the gift by deducting the present value of the payments you receive from the total value of the trust assets.

The value of the gift is determined by the annuity payment amount, the length of the trust term, and the interest rate used in the IRS tables. The value of the gift can be such as to make the value of the current gift to be equal or close to zero.

CHAPTER 26 Grantor Retained Annuity Trusts (GRATs)

GRAT Example 1

A 70-year-old client and spouse transfer $1 million to a GRAT in order to remove the principal and future appreciation from their estate. The IRS assesses the value of the $1 million asset at less than $600,000. This provides a 40% discount on the size of the gift and therefore saves, if the gift tax rate is 35%, approximately $140,000 in gift tax.

GRAT Example 2

Assume that a 60-year-old client transfers a $1 million asset to the trust. The IRS interest rate is 5.8%, the term of the trust is 10 years, with an 8% annual growth of the principal, and an annuity payout of $50,000 per year. We'll also assume that the trust produces no income.

Based on these assumptions, the current taxable gift would be $628,485. If the gift tax rate is 35% that would require $219,970 in taxes. On the other hand, if the client uses some of his lifetime gift tax exemption, he may not have to pay any actual gift tax.

By removing that $1 million asset from his estate, along with 10 years of growth at 8%, he will save over $700,000 in estate taxes with the GRAT. After accounting for the gift taxes, he would still have net tax savings of around $480,000.

During the term of the GRAT, the client would have received $500,000 in annuity payments, and his beneficiaries would receive approximately $1.4 million at the end of the trust term.

> The GRAT is typically used when you have an asset that you expect to appreciate significantly, and which you will want to eventually pass on to the beneficiaries.

CHAPTER 26   Grantor Retained Annuity Trusts (GRATs)

Things to Consider When Using a GRAT

Like many of the sophisticated planning tools, the GRAT is not without planning realities to consider. As you consider using a GRAT, please keep in mind the following facts:

- Because the GRAT is irrevocable, you lose control over the trust assets.

- This is a "grantor trust" which means that you will still be responsible for income taxes on all trust income, whether or not it is actually distributed. For this reason, GRATs are normally invested for capital appreciation rather than income.

- If you die before the expiration of the trust term, the full value of the assets will still be included in your estate. Therefore, the term should never be set at a point that is longer than your life expectancy.

- There are several costs entailed with GRAT setup, administration, accounting, appraisal, and trustee's fees.

The GRAT can be a powerful tool in your estate plan to reduce both gift and estate taxes. As you can see from the examples above, there are several factors to be considered when establishing a GRAT, and they should only be undertaken with help from your expert advisors.

CHAPTER 27

Self-Cancelling Installment Notes (SCINs)

Another way to pass money to the next generation with minimal taxes

Overview

A self-cancelling installment note (SCIN) is similar to an installment sale. The owner sells his or her business or other asset to a family member taking back a promissory note. The entire note balance is forgiven if the seller dies before the note is paid in full. It has the potential to significantly reduce estate taxes. In order for the technique to be valid, the buyer must pay a premium for the self-cancelling attribute.

The terms of a SCIN must:

- Clearly state the selling price.

- Have a selling price based on a formally appraised value.

- State a fair market rate of interest on the note.

- Specify the term of the note and the payment amounts.

- Be secured by an interest in the business or asset.

CHAPTER 27 Self-Cancelling Installment Notes (SCINs)

How it Works

In essence, the SCIN is a cross between a private annuity and an installment sale and has many of the advantages of both. A SCIN involves the sale of a business interest, stock, real estate, or some other asset, typically to one or more family members in exchange for an installment note. In essence, you become a "friendly banker" by financing the sale of a family business, family farm, or other asset through a loan payable by your children, grandchildren, or others in installments over a specified period of years. The SCIN can be designed to require monthly, quarterly, or annual payments.

But unlike the classic installment sale, the note in a SCIN includes provisions for automatic cancellation of the unpaid balance at the death of the seller. In other words the SCIN is a promissory note (evidence of debt), given by a buyer to a seller, with a provision under which the obligation to make any future payments ends at the seller's death. If the seller lives beyond the period over which installment payments are to be made, the "cancel at death" provision is ignored. If the seller dies during the term of the note, the buyer's obligation to make payments ends on the date of death.

> This is a tool that can be used by a donor in poor health. The earlier into the specified term the seller dies, the more advantageous the SCIN becomes.

Your goal is to keep the unpaid balance of the note out of your estate, and avoid any gift tax on the transfer.

Although it is unpleasant to point out, the ideal candidate for a SCIN has a shorter actual life span than would be indicated by actuarial tables that predict life expectancy. This is a tool that can be used by a donor in poor health. The earlier into the specified term the seller dies, the more advantageous the SCIN is. This is because the property transferred plus all the appreciation and any income it has produced is removed from the transferor's estate. Only the loan payments received and unspent at the seller's death are included in the estate.

CHAPTER 27 Self-Cancelling Installment Notes (SCINs)

Advantages of a SCIN

Pay capital gains tax over time instead of all at once. You can sell an asset with a low tax basis and spread the gain over the term of the note rather than bunching that gain all into one year. Prorating the taxable gain over the payment period may enable a shift of income from higher-bracket tax years (such as when you are employed) to lower-bracket years (such as after retirement).

Save estate tax on asset appreciation. If the business or other asset purchased by the children appreciates after the sale, you have in essence created an "estate freeze" on the sold assets since your estate will remain the same size if you spend the loan payments each year for costs of living.

Create cash flow. If you own non-income-producing assets (such as undeveloped land or a family vacation home) the use of a SCIN can keep the asset within the family, yet increase the seller's income significantly. Children who anticipate the need to support aging parents may want to consider this "graceful and dignified" approach to provide income for their parents who might otherwise be financially burdened. A fixed stream of income for the term of the note is secured (assuming the buyer-child remains both financially able and willing to make payments).

CHAPTER 28

The Advantages of Being a U.S. Citizen in Estate Planning

Be aware of the planning pitfalls if you (or your spouse) are not a U.S. citizen.

Background

When a marriage is between U.S. citizens, each spouse may give away during life, or pass at death, an unlimited amount of assets to one another. This is called the "unlimited marital deduction." This deduction is important and helpful in "balancing assets" between husband and wife in the estate planning process, thus ensuring that each of their individual exemption amounts are used to the fullest extent possible.

Prior to the Technical and Miscellaneous Revenue Act of 1988 (TAMRA), a U.S. Citizen or Resident was allowed an unlimited Marital Deduction for both the federal estate and gift tax, regardless of the spouse's citizenship.

Congress was concerned, however, that a non-citizen spouse would give up their U.S. residency after the citizen spouse passed away, returning to their home country, and taking all the deceased spouse's assets with them, avoiding U.S. taxes. TAMRA's goal was to stop that from happening.

CHAPTER 28 The Advantages of Being a U.S. Citizen in Estate Planning

Current Situation

Today, citizens and legal residents of the United States are subject to gift and estate taxes on all their assets worldwide. There is no unlimited marital deduction for transfers from a citizen spouse to a non-citizen spouse.

"Non-resident aliens" are subject to U.S. gift and estate tax on assets "situated in the United States." Double taxation is possible since every country applies different rules to determine the taxpayer's legal domicile. The United States currently has a tax treaty that affects gift and estate taxes with 17 countries: Australia, Austria, Canada, Denmark, Germany, Finland, France, Greece, Ireland, Italy, Japan, The Netherlands, Norway, South Africa, Sweden, Switzerland, and the United Kingdom.

Considerations for Non-citizens

"Green card" holders have permanent residency in the United States which allows for easy travel in and out of the country. However, green card holders will be subject to income tax on their worldwide assets, even if they are not living in the U.S. They will also be exposed to gift and estate taxes on all their assets, regardless of in which country the assets are held.

By giving up a green card a person is considered a nonresident alien, but the IRS will still tax the person as if they were a resident when it comes to income tax. For estate taxes, however, that same person will only be taxed on assets held in the United States.

Since a person can be determined to be a resident for income tax purposes, and a nonresident for estate tax purposes, special planning is needed to prevent a "tax train wreck" both during life and upon death.

CHAPTER 28 The Advantages of Being a U.S. Citizen in Estate Planning

Current Laws Regarding Lifetime Transfers from a Citizen to a Non-Citizen Spouse

Gifts up to the annual exclusion amount ($14,000 in 2013, indexed for inflation) can be made to a spouse during life without a gift tax, even if the spouse is a non-citizen. And even though two citizen spouses could give an unlimited amount to each other every year without gift taxes, the citizen spouse can gift no more than $143,000 (in 2013, indexed for inflation) annually to a non-citizen spouse without gift tax consequences. Note that these types of gifts between a citizen and non-citizen spouse may be encouraged as a planning device to reduce the impact of the marital deduction restrictions at death.

The Qualified Domestic Trust (QDOT)

At death, gifts to the non-citizen spouse can qualify for the marital deduction, and thus postpone estate tax, only if the property is held in a Qualified Domestic Trust (QDOT). Again, the underlying purpose for this requirement is to ensure collection of the estate tax on the death of the non-citizen spouse, and keep the surviving spouse from removing the assets from the United States and thus deprive the IRS of its eventual "inheritance."

How it Works

Your will or trust may provide an outright gift on your death to your non-citizen spouse. If that is your choice, you should also include an option for your spouse to "disclaim" part or all of the outright gift, causing the assets to instead pass to a QDOT for your spouse's benefit.

By disclaiming that gift, your spouse will have several options:

- Become a U.S. citizen – but this must be done before the estate tax is filed

CHAPTER 28   The Advantages of Being a U.S. Citizen in Estate Planning

- Pay the tax – but this is only appropriate for a spouse who plans to leave the U.S.

- Establish the QDOT

Requirements of a QDOT

The QDOT has several requirements:

- The QDOT must have at least one trustee who is a U.S. citizen or a U.S. corporation

- The trustee must be able to withhold taxes due on any distributions of the trust principal

- The executor of the estate must make the QDOT election to qualify for the marital deduction

- If QDOT assets exceed $2,000,000 (large QDOT) the U.S. trustee must be a bank, or the individual U.S. trustee must furnish a bond or letter of credit to the U.S. Treasury for 65% of the value of the QDOT assets at the first spouse's death

- If QDOT assets are less than $2 million, the large QDOT requirements are only needed if the amount of the real property located outside the U.S. accounts for more than 35% of all trust assets

> Citizens and legal residents of the United States are subject to gift and estate taxes on all their assets worldwide. There is no unlimited marital deduction for transfers from a citizen spouse to a non-citizen spouse.

CHAPTER 28   The Advantages of Being a U.S. Citizen in Estate Planning

Taxation of Assets Held in a QDOT

The QDOT defers taxation of the assets within it until one of three things happens:

- The death of the surviving non-citizen spouse
- Distributions of trust principal
- Termination of a trust as a QDOT

Income paid to the non-citizen spouse is taxed as regular income under the normal income tax rules. If any principal is paid out, those assets are taxed as if they were included in the deceased citizen spouse's estate.

At the death of the non-citizen spouse, the assets remaining in the QDOT are subject to the federal estate tax as though they were included in the estate of the deceased citizen spouse (and are not included in the non-citizen spouse's estate). Of course, any appreciation in the value of the assets would also be subject to tax upon the non-citizen spouse's death.

There are special considerations with jointly held property, and there are ways to use life insurance to avoid the non-citizen spouse problem. Each case is unique and will require review by your attorney and advisory team.

CHAPTER 29

Asset Protection

Keeping it in the family after you're gone

Goal of Asset Protection Planning

The goal of asset protection planning is to change a creditor's economic analysis. We want to remove the incentive for anyone to sue you, and increase the ability to force an early settlement. In order to properly understand asset protection, one must analyze your sources of liability, timing, the creditor, and the specific assets under consideration.

Some of the potential sources of liability our clients face include divorce, auto liability, liability from owning real estate, negligence, the liability of others (minor children, employees, etc), professional malpractice, liability as an Officer or Director, and contractual liability.

Understanding Asset Protection

First of all, asset protection is not about hiding assets. It doesn't work. Private investigators may find the assets. They will be found out in a debtor examination. Perjuring oneself is never a viable option.

Secondly, creditors can only go after assets that you actually own. The strategy is to remove title of the asset from your name but still allow you to have control and enjoyment of those assets. The way this is usually done is through limited

CHAPTER 29   Asset Protection

liability companies and trusts. With respect to certain limited liability companies, there is no remedy to attach a membership interest. In certain states, the only thing a creditor can obtain is a charging order that says the creditor can collect from income that is paid out of the LLC. The creditor cannot force a distribution. Thus, it makes it difficult for the creditor to get to the asset. This makes settlement much more favorable to the debtor.

The third concept is that certain assets are exempt depending on the State in which you live. For example, Texas, Kansas, Florida, and Nevada have desirable homestead protection. In other States, like Florida, annuities and life insurance are protected by statute and court decision.

> The goal of asset protection planning is to change a creditor's economic analysis. You want to remove the incentive for anyone to sue you, and increase the ability to force an early settlement.

Another goal in asset protection is to make assets less desirable. An example of this would be placing liens on real estate. For example, one could create a home equity line of credit from a family member and secure it with a deed of trust.

Along the way, you must carefully consider whether a court will view a transfer as a fraudulent conveyance to defraud creditors. Asset protection is designed to protect against future potential creditors, not current existing creditors, or people you reasonably expect may become creditors.

Estate Planning and Financial Planning

Asset protection is best done as part of an overall estate and financial plan. Things to consider include:

- How much money do you need to retire?
- How much money do you need to maintain your current lifestyle?
- What are your sources of current and future cash flow?

CHAPTER 29   Asset Protection

- Are these sources protected or unprotected from creditors?

- How much do you want to pass on after you're gone?

Brilliant financial and estate plans can be rendered worthless if your assets are taken by a judgment creditor before the plans can be implemented.

The single most important thing about asset protection is that you not leave an inheritance outright! By leaving an inheritance to your loved ones in a protective trust, you can provide asset protection for them that they cannot provide for themselves.

CHAPTER 30

Asset Protection – Domestic Techniques

Why leave yourself unprotected during life – penny wise and dollar foolish

There are several techniques for asset protection using existing United States laws and common practices.

Liability Insurance

Liability insurance should be considered as the first line of defense in a comprehensive asset protection plan. Creditors consider liability insurance to be "easy money" since it can be readily collected. In addition, liability insurance offers an incentive to settle early, particularly if the client's assets are unreachable or expensive to pursue.

Types of insurance you might consider include homeowner's, property and casualty, umbrella insurance, auto, general business, professional liability, and officers and directors insurance.

Nonetheless, liability insurance should not be relied upon as the sole source of asset protection. Judgments can be rendered in excess of your insurance limits, and all insurance policies have multiple built-in exclusions.

CHAPTER 30   Asset Protection – Domestic Techniques

State and Federal Bankruptcy Laws and Homestead Exemptions

Historically, state property laws determine the types and values of property that a debtor may withhold from creditors in bankruptcy. However, the 2005 Bankruptcy Act curtails the ability of filers to take advantage of their state property exemptions. The Act prevents a debtor from claiming a state's exemptions unless they have lived in the same jurisdiction for at least two years before filing for bankruptcy.

One of the most important state laws pertains to homestead exemptions. These types of exemptions are based on the public policy that the family home is sacred, regardless of the financial condition of the owner. In Florida, for example, a property of ½ acre or less inside city limits, or a property up to 160 acres outside city limits, can be protected in a bankruptcy proceeding.

Under the 2005 Bankruptcy Act, the individual state homestead exemptions may not exceed $125,000 for any property acquired within 1215 days before filing the bankruptcy petition.

Protecting Retirement Plan Assets

Retirement plans which are generally protected include those covered under ERISA (the Employee Retirement Security Act of 1974) and the "anti-alienation" rule. Plans that are protected include profit sharing plans, money purchase plans, 401(k) plans, 403(b) plans to which employers make contributions, and defined benefit plans. Further, protections were enhanced with certain limitations for IRAs after 2005 based both on court cases and on the provisions of the Bankruptcy Abuse Prevention and Consumer Protection Act of 2005 (BAPCPA). However, these protections for IRAs are also very sensitive to applicable state law, so one must exercise care. Note that while these plans may be protected for the owner and spouse, they are not necessarily protected for non-spousal beneficiaries unless you use an IRA Inheritance Trust as described in Chapter 13.

CHAPTER 30   Asset Protection – Domestic Techniques

Life Insurance

The death benefit paid to a beneficiary passes free from the claims of the insured's creditors. However, the death benefit paid to a beneficiary will be subject to the claims of the beneficiary's creditors, unless the proceeds pass to a discretionary spendthrift trust for the beneficiary.

The cash surrender value of a life insurance policy cannot be reached by a creditor of the insured. The insured can withdraw some or all of the cash value and spend it without interference from creditors.

> Leaving yourself unprotected during life is penny wise and dollar foolish!

Annuities

The proceeds of a fixed annuity cannot be attached, garnished, or otherwise reached by the creditors of the annuitant or the beneficiary who will receive the remaining annuity payments upon the death of the annuitant.

The proceeds of a variable annuity cannot be reached by the annuitant's creditors prior to the maturity date. Nor can the proceeds be reached by the creditors of the beneficiary who will receive the remaining payments of the variable annuity.

Annuity payments can retain their protected status so long as the funds can be properly traced and are not commingled with unprotected assets.

Business Entities

To understand the benefit of using business entities for asset protection, it is helpful to understand the difference between inside and outside liability. Inside liability results from something related to the actual assets or activities of the business entity. Outside liability results from something unrelated to the assets or activities of the business entity.

CHAPTER 30   Asset Protection – Domestic Techniques

Inside liability can be contained within a business entity, thereby protecting all assets outside the entity from liability. For example, if you own a rental property within a business entity, such as Rental Property, Inc. and somebody slips and falls on the property, your only asset at risk is the property itself. Your home, bank accounts, investment accounts, and other personal assets outside the rental property corporation are safe.

Trusts

Trusts that are created by one person (called the grantor or trustmaker) for the benefit of another person (called the beneficiary) can be drafted to include creditor protection for the beneficiary.

For example, you might create a "discretionary spendthrift trust" that restricts the beneficiaries' ability to transfer, sell, or otherwise give away any of their rights in the trust. In a spendthrift trust, the Trustee has uncontrolled discretion whether or not to make distributions to the beneficiary from the trust. Therefore, a creditor of the beneficiary cannot compel the Trustee to make distributions.

You can and should create a discretionary spendthrift trust for a spouse, children, and other beneficiaries. You also want to encourage your parents or others from whom you expect to receive an inheritance to establish a discretionary spendthrift trust to hold your inheritance and keep it protected from your creditors.

Domestic Asset Protection Trusts (DAPTs)

The Domestic Asset Protection Trust (DAPT) is a trust that is formed in one of several states having anti-creditor trust statutes that allow Self-Settled Spendthrift Trusts – trusts that allow you to establish a trust for yourself which will protect you from creditors. Alaska was the first state to enact an anti-creditor trust act, followed by Delaware, Nevada, Rhode Island, Utah, and Wyoming. In 2010, Wyoming became the first state to give creditor protection to single member LLCs. Most of the DAPT legislation is the same from state to state, and usually includes:

CHAPTER 30   Asset Protection – Domestic Techniques

- The ability to form a trust for your own benefit that will protect you against your creditors; something that is typically prohibited by public policy in all the other states.

- A shortened period of time for a creditor to challenge a transfer to one of these trusts.

- Terms that make it more difficult for a creditor to prove that a transfer to the trust was a fraudulent transfer.

In Wyoming, some clients are using a Wyoming DAPT as the owner of a Wyoming Close LLC, thus protecting the income stream from the LLC. This combination has become known as the "Cowboy Cocktail," and if properly structured, can provide some of the best domestic asset protection available in the United States.

Summary

The more sources of liability you have, the more important it is that you develop a comprehensive asset protection plan.

While an asset protection plan is designed to protect assets from loss, and decrease the possibility of being the target of a lawsuit, you cannot hide assets, defraud existing creditors, or avoid paying U.S. income taxes.

Therefore, any comprehensive asset protection plan is better positioned to succeed if established before any incident occurs that leads to liability.

CHAPTER 30   Asset Protection – Domestic Techniques

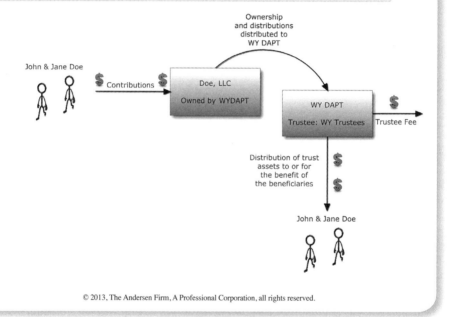

CHAPTER 30 Asset Protection – Domestic Techniques

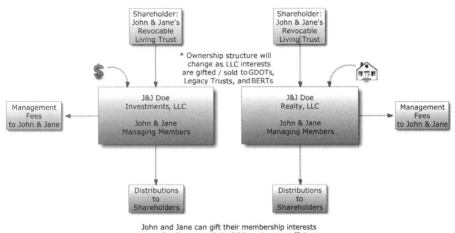

CHAPTER 31

Asset Protection – Offshore Techniques

Avoiding the uncertainties of U.S. courts

In spite of all the possible asset protection techniques available in the United States, our courts (particularly bankruptcy courts) can be unpredictable. Clients sometimes choose to avail themselves of offshore planning techniques.

Offshore planning is simply planning under the laws of another country. People from Europe or Asia who do planning in the United States are actually doing offshore planning. You might make use of an asset protection trust (APT) – which is a foreign grantor trust whose trustee is not required to honor U.S. judgments. Cook Island Trusts and Nevis Trusts currently rank at the top for asset protection purposes. The actual assets may be placed in an LLC of a different country such as Cook Islands or Nevis with the assets invested in jurisdictions such as Switzerland or Lichtenstein.

If you decide to use offshore planning, you need to keep sufficient assets outside of the offshore planning structures to pay your anticipated living expenses for the foreseeable future. Our clients who use offshore planning techniques usually have at least $1,000,000 to protect, and/or are in a high-risk profession or business.

The idea is to protect a "nest egg" so that in a worst case scenario where you are wiped out financially, you still have a protected nest egg with which to start over. If you were to transfer all your assets offshore, thereby leaving yourself insolvent, the courts are more likely to characterize the transfer as a fraudulent conveyance.

Taxation of Offshore Trusts

Generally, U.S. residents are subject to taxation on their worldwide income. The fact that assets are in a foreign trust that is protected from creditors does not change this. Asset protection trusts are not designed to reduce taxes, and income they earn is taxable, just as it would have been if it were earned in the U.S.

There are additional IRS reporting requirements for assets in an offshore trust. These additional requirements mandate that the amount of assets in the trust is disclosed, information about the trustee is disclosed, the country where the trustee is domiciled is listed, and a reporting of the income earned on these assets. These additional reporting requirements have increased since the passage of The Patriot Act, and other laws designed to reduce money laundering and other financial crimes.

The Domestic/Offshore Hybrid

This type of trust typically keeps your asset accounts in the United States, but based on a triggering event, moves your nest egg to a previously prepared offshore entity and jurisdiction.

Advantages of Offshore Planning

Remember that offshore asset protection planning is not about hiding assets. If you lose a major lawsuit, you will have to declare, under oath, the value and location of all your assets including offshore business entities and trusts. Instead, offshore planning is about creating solid barriers so you become an

CHAPTER 31   Asset Protection – Offshore Techniques

undesirable target to a creditor or "predator." The advantages of using international planning include:

> *Offshore planning helps you to avoid the vagaries of U.S. Courts.*

- Many international jurisdictions have strict secrecy laws, so that even if you disclose the location of a bank account, for example, the banker cannot verify its existence under penalty of law.

- International courts in many countries are not required to recognize the judgments from other countries. So even though a creditor won a lawsuit against you in the United States, they may have to initiate a new action against you in the offshore jurisdiction.

- If they bring a lawsuit in the offshore jurisdiction, they will be required to hire attorneys who are licensed in that jurisdiction.

- Many jurisdictions require foreign plaintiffs to post a bond or cash deposit when filing the lawsuit, because they will award attorneys fees and court costs to the winner, and want to be sure the plaintiff will be able to cover those costs if he loses.

- Most foreign jurisdictions require a higher standard of proof for a judgment.

- Most foreign jurisdictions have a presumption against fraudulent transfers and require the plaintiff to prove a fraudulent transfer, rather than you having to prove that there was no fraudulent transfer.

- Some foreign jurisdictions provide that even if a part of a transfer is determined to be fraudulent then the trust and all other assets within it will still remain protected.

- Foreign countries often require a shorter period of time after transfer before the transferred assets are protected, and some will protect even fraudulent transfers if they are not challenged within a certain amount of time (e.g. two years) after transfer.

CHAPTER 31   Asset Protection – Offshore Techniques

- And if all those protections aren't enough, your offshore trust can contain instructions that if the trust is breached, all assets should immediately be transferred to a new trust in a different country – thus starting the process all over again for the creditor.

- When faced with these very real obstacles, most creditors are willing to settle for the amount offered by liability insurance coverage.

Like all other advanced planning strategies, you don't want to involve yourself in offshore planning without experienced counsel. In the Bahamas alone, there are over 500 banks and trust companies, some of which are 200-year-old European entities, and others who are little more than a nameplate on an office door. And some offshore jurisdictions will be much more appropriate for your individual circumstances than others. Always seek professional guidance.

CHAPTER 32

The Secret of Discounts for Gifting

The "Freeze & Squeeze" technique

When it comes to gift taxes, the IRS rules say that a gift is valued at its "fair market value" which is the price it would bring "between a willing buyer and a willing seller, neither being under any compulsion to buy or to sell, and both having reasonable knowledge of relevant facts." That is, the gift is worth whatever you could exchange it for on the open market. That valuation applies to both lifetime gifts and valuation at death for determination of estate taxes.

The idea behind the "freeze and squeeze" technique is to "squeeze" that value to reduce gift taxes, and to "freeze" the valuation and allow subsequent growth to happen outside the taxable estate.

To implement this strategy, a client will usually incorporate a business entity of some type such as a Family Limited Liability Company (FLLC) or a Family Limited Partnership (FLP) as part of their estate plan. For purposes of this explanation, let's assume you choose to use the LLC.

How It Works

- You contribute the property or assets you want to pass on to your loved ones into the LLC in exchange for ownership interests in the LLC. (For example, you might transfer $1 million in securities

CHAPTER 32   The Secret of Discounts for Gifting

to the LLC in exchange for LLC "shares" representing 100% ownership of the LLC. The LLC would presumably be worth $1 million.)

- Next, you decide to give some of the shares in the LLC to your children to reduce the size of your taxable estate. Let's say you give 25% of the LLC to your son, and another 25% to your daughter – leaving you with 50% ownership in the LLC.

- It seems logical that if the LLC has $1 million in assets, the share belonging to each of your children would be worth $250,000 – and that would be the value of the gift upon which you might pay gift taxes. But the "freeze and squeeze" technique will change that logic.

- The LLC agreement contains specific terms that say no matter how much of the LLC you give away, you still retain total control of the management of the LLC. You make all the investment decisions. You control if and when distributions might be made from the LLC. For your children, that's called "lack of control."

> The "freeze and squeeze" technique allows you to give away more during life and at death, without incurring gift or estate taxes.

- Next, the LLC agreement also says that the person to whom you give LLC shares cannot sell or transfer those shares. Neither can they use their shares as collateral for a loan – unless you give permission. In other words, the children are totally dependent on you to get any money out of the LLC. For your children that's called a "lack of liquidity" or a "lack of marketability."

- These special LLC terms are what create the discounts that you seek in the freeze and squeeze technique. How much would somebody pay on the open market for your son's or daughter's LLC shares? Remember – that's the definition of "fair market value." Assuming you give permission to your son to sell his LLC shares, a buyer certainly wouldn't pay your son $250,000

CHAPTER 32   The Secret of Discounts for Gifting

because the buyer would have the same problems your son has – lack of control and lack of marketability. The shares are therefore worth something less than $250,000.

- So how do you determine what these shares are really worth? The determination is made by a qualified independent business appraiser. The appraiser will take the underlying value of the assets, and then apply a lack of control discount, AND a lack of marketability discount.

- Let's say the appraiser comes up with a combined discount totaling 33%. That means the gifts you gave your son and daughter are really worth only $167,500 each instead of $250,000. That reduces the amount of gift tax due accordingly.

- On the flip side, if you want to give an amount that matches your lifetime gift tax exemption, you'll be able to actually give considerably more than that amount when the discounts are applied, thereby reducing the size of your estate even further.

- Of course, once these gifts are given to the children, they are out of your estate, and any future growth of those assets is also out of your estate.

- The restrictions in the LLC agreement keep you in control of everything.

- IMPORTANT NOTE: These restrictions that work so well to discount the value of the gift also work against you by increasing the value of the portion of the LLC you keep (called a "premium" instead of a discount). To minimize the impact, many of our clients choose to give away much, if not all, of the LLC in non-voting shares with the restrictions in place, keeping only 1% ownership – but still having all the control. That way, at the time of death, if that 1% has an actual value of $10,000, the premium adjustment will make it worth $13,300 – not much of an impact on the estate size for tax purposes.

As with the other advanced strategies, the "freeze and squeeze" technique requires the active involvement of your professional advisory team.

CHAPTER 33

Divorce and Estate Planning

The pitfalls of divorce, separation, and beneficiary designations

Things are rarely simple when it comes to divorce, and that is definitely the case when you consider its impact on your estate planning. It is extremely important to have your estate plan reviewed and updated after divorce.

There are several considerations:

- State law may revoke a will or certain provisions within it in the case of divorce

- You must change a former spouse's designation as your executor or personal representative, trustee, attorney under a power of attorney, heath care agent, and as beneficiary in life insurance policies and retirement plans.

- Unless your parents have done proper estate planning, the divorce court may consider your expected inheritance when determining property settlements, alimony, etc. Future or contingent inheritances are generally not reachable, but some courts have considered them when proper planning was not in place.

- Current interests in trust are generally not reachable if the trust has a spendthrift provision, but that varies by jurisdiction.

CHAPTER 33   Divorce and Estate Planning

Planning Solutions in the Event of Divorce

Alimony Trusts – The objective of an alimony trust is to protect the recipient spouse and end interaction between the spouses. Once the amount of funding is determined by the court, it is paid to an irrevocable trust, which pays out to the recipient spouse. The recipient spouse is taxed on the income received.

Structuring Tax-Free Property Settlements – This type of settlement provides for income tax-free property transfers incident to divorce. Lifetime transfers between spouses motivated by divorce result in the recipient spouse receiving the basis and holding period of the transferor spouse. Transfers in satisfaction of support and alimony obligations, or made under a tax-free settlement agreement or court order, are not considered a gift, and are not subject to gift taxes. Settlements must be drafted in compliance with the tax code to qualify.

Capital Gains on the Sale of a Primary Residence

The sale of a primary residence has a general exclusion from tax on the property's capital gains up to $250,000 for an individual and up to $500,000 for a married couple as long as it was owned and used as a primary residence for 2 of the previous 5 years. In order to take advantage of the full $500,000 exclusion, the couple should sell the home prior to the divorce.

For example, assume a husband and wife purchased a home some time ago for $200,000 and it is now valued at $700,000. Husband and wife have owned and used the home for more than 2 of the previous 5 years, and are now getting divorced. If the husband transfers his interest to the wife and she later sells, she will only get the $250,000 exclusion and will pay capital gains tax on the other $250,000 when she later sells the house. If the husband and wife sell prior to the divorce, they will get the $500,000 exclusion and no capital gains tax will be due.

In a sale of the primary residence after a divorce, there are several considerations to determine who qualifies as the "owner" when calculating the requirements to meet the exclusion.

CHAPTER 33   Divorce and Estate Planning

Handling Stock Options and Deferred Compensation

Many courts hold that stock options are a form of income rather than property. If they are property, the ex-spouse has no future claim to them. If they are considered income, the stock options are eligible for alimony and child support computation.

Revenue Ruling (2002-22) held that:

- An employee spouse, who transfers interests in nonqualified stock options and nonqualified deferred compensation to his former spouse incident to divorce, is not required to include the amount in gross income upon the transfer.

- The former spouse is required to include the amount in gross income when he or she exercises the stock options or when the deferred compensation is paid or made available to the former spouse.

Another Revenue Ruling (2004-60) held that:

- Nonqualified stock options and deferred compensation transferred by an employee to a former spouse incident to a divorce are subject to FICA, FUTA, and income tax withholding to the same extent as if retained by the employee.

- It is payable at the time the non-employee spouse exercises the options or receives payments under the deferred compensation plan, not when they are transferred to the non-employee spouse.

Retirement Plans and Divorce

Qualified Pension Plans – A Qualified Domestic Relations Order (QDRO) is required. That is a judgment, decree, or order pursuant to a state's domestic relations law. It can provide for the spouse to be an alternative payee. Very specific rules apply, and failure to follow them can result in immediate tax or jeopardize the plan. The spouse is taxed on receipt of money from the plan, but the 10% early distribution penalty is waived. The alternate payee can also roll the proceeds to his or her own IRA.

Individual Retirement Accounts (IRAs) – A QDRO is not required. The transfer of an IRA is not taxable if it's pursuant to a divorce decree or a written agreement. After transfer, the recipient spouse is treated as the owner of the IRA with regular tax treatment. The recipient spouse can also name their own beneficiaries.

Life Insurance and Divorce

In a divorce the divorcing spouse still has an insurable interest in the other. In fact, life insurance is often used to protect the income of a spouse paying alimony or child support. Divorce courts will sometimes require the providing spouse to maintain a life insurance policy that will cover the support payments for however long the payments have been ordered to be made.

One issue to be discussed is who will be considered the owner of the policy. The owner has control of the cash value and beneficiary designations.

> Divorce impacts your estate plan in many ways. It is extremely important to have your plan reviewed and updated after divorce.

Other Considerations

There are several other planning considerations in the event of a divorce. For example, you and your financial advisors must consider the impact on investment strategies and outcomes, joint tax returns will no longer be used, changes must be made to existing charitable trusts, etc. The most important step is to undergo a thorough and professional review of your estate planning strategies and documents by your professional advisory team, including beneficiary designations.

CHAPTER 34

Charitable Planning

If you have a charitable passion there are many choices on how to give

When people think about charitable giving in the context of estate and financial planning, they often think in terms of tax savings. History shows that charity generally starts at home, but it also shows that the people of America are the most generous in the world. Most of them give for truly philanthropic reasons – thinking of tax savings as an extra benefit. In other words, many would still contribute even if it did not save them taxes. That being said, you should still be aware of the charitable tax rules.

Does My Contribution Qualify for Income Tax Deductions?

By definition, a charitable contribution is a:

- current payment
- made to a qualified charitable organization
- with donative intent
- in excess of the value of any benefit received by the donor.

A charitable contribution is deductible when an unconditional gift is delivered to a charitable organization. If the contribution is made by check, it is deductible when the check is mailed (as long as it clears.) Therefore, a check mailed on

> *History shows that charity generally starts at home, but it also shows that the people of America are the most generous in the world.*

December 31st will still be deductible for that calendar year, even though the charity won't receive it until after January 1st of the new year. In order for a deduction to be allowed, the donor must prove that the contribution was actually made, and substantiate its value.

How Much Can I Deduct?

You cannot deduct 100% of your income with charitable deductions. Instead, you can deduct a percentage of your Adjusted Gross Income (AGI) depending on the type of charity and the type of property donated.

If you donate cash to a public charity you get a deduction up to 50% of AGI, but a gift to a private charity is limited to 30% of AGI. If instead you contribute capital gain property, you get a deduction up to 30% of AGI for a public charity and 20% for a private charity. When it comes to gift and estate taxes, there is no difference between public and private charities, and no percentage limitation.

Charitable Planning For Life and Death

In the big scheme of things, there are three possible heirs in any estate plan – family and loved ones, the IRS, or charity. During life, charitable contributions can be made outright or in trust. The contribution will generally reduce current income taxes based on a percentage of adjusted gross income and the type of property transferred. The gift to qualified charities will be removed from your estate and thereby reduce estate taxes. Also, if contributions are made to charitable trusts during your lifetime, there may be an income stream to you and your spouse with the remainder going to charity at the second death.

Also, it is possible to leave property in a charitable trust at death, whereby the income from the property goes to the named charity for a period of years, with the remainder going to the heirs estate tax free. All of this can be accomplished by using advanced estate planning tools and techniques discussed in more detail in the chapters that follow. Again, all charitable planning begins with your goals and objectives, not with tax considerations alone.

Several charitable techniques are discussed in the chapters that follow: Direct Gifts to Charity (35); Charitable Annuity Trusts and Unitrusts (36); Private Foundations (37); Community Foundations and Donor Advised Funds (38); and Charitable Annuities (39).

CHAPTER 35

Direct Gifts to Charity

Beware of the downside of direct gifts to both your money and the charity

Almost any asset can be easily contributed to a charity, and different gifts have different deductibility rules.

If you contribute cash, securities, real estate, or business interests, your deduction is equal to the fair market value of the asset contributed. If you can't use the whole deduction in the current year (because of AGI limits), you can carry the deduction forward for up to five years.

If the gift is an automobile, boat, or airplane, the rules are a little different. The amount of the deduction is based upon the use of the property by the charitable organization, the condition of the property, and other factors. If the property is used in a significant manner by the charity, or the charity makes a material improvement to the property before selling it, a deduction is allowed for the full fair market value of the property. If it's sold without any significant improvements, the deduction is limited to the price received by the charity.

You can make a direct gift of a life insurance policy by naming the charity as the beneficiary. You won't get a current income tax deduction because the charity won't benefit until they receive the death proceeds of the policy. If you own the policy, it will still be included in your taxable estate, but because the charity is named as the beneficiary, the full amount of the proceeds can be deducted.

CHAPTER 35   Direct Gifts to Charity

Disadvantages of Direct Gifts

Direct gifts to charity tend to be less part of a comprehensive plan, and more of a spontaneous act of generosity. That's not always the best way to approach philanthropy – for you or for the charity.

Non-profit organizations usually receive cash gifts through some sort of direct marketing activities. Fundraising costs money and spontaneous gifts are, by definition, unpredictable. This means that many charities that rely on cash income, and those who cannot afford a direct marketing campaign, are likely to lead a "hand-to-mouth" existence. It is ultimately better for the charity to have a steady, predictable source of income with which to run its programs, and that results most often from longer term planned giving programs.

> Beware of the downside of direct gifts to charity – your gift can create a disincentive for the charity to raise money.

The disadvantage of direct gifts for you is that it reduces the income or assets you have available to live on, it could mean leaving less to your family, and it may not maximize the gift from a tax perspective.

CHAPTER 36

Charitable Annuity Trusts and Unitrusts

Ways to provide for the kids, give to charity, and save taxes

Charitable trusts of all kinds involve what is known as "split interest" gifts. That is, part of the interest in the asset goes to you or your beneficiaries, and part goes to charity. Typically, one beneficiary gets the trust income and the other the trust remainder. The two most common types of charitable trusts are the Charitable Remainder Trust and the Charitable Lead Trust.

Charitable Remainder Annuity Trusts and Unitrusts (CRATs and CRUTs): You or a Beneficiary Get the Annual Payment, the Charity Gets the Remainder

How They Work

Both the CRAT and the CRUT are irrevocable trusts which provide for an annual payment to a non-charitable beneficiary or beneficiaries, with the remainder of the trust property distributed to the charity upon the death of the last income beneficiary.

CHAPTER 36   Charitable Annuity Trusts and Unitrusts

With the CRAT, a fixed dollar amount or percentage of the initial value of the trust assets is paid to the non-charitable beneficiary annually. The payment to the income beneficiary remains level for the entire term of the CRAT. Also, a CRAT may receive only one contribution. No additional property may be added to the trust. This type of trust is most appropriate for older donors who require a steady income and are not worried about future inflation.

With the CRUT, a fixed percentage of the value of the trust assets is paid to the non-charitable beneficiary annually, with the assets being revalued each year. With this type of trust, the amount of the distributions to the income beneficiaries will fluctuate each year, based on the value of the trust. CRUTs allow for additional contributions of property after the initial contribution.

A NIMCRUT (Net Income with Make-up Charitable Remainder Unitrust) is a variant of the standard CRUT. This variant still provides for distribution of a certain percentage of the trust's assets, revalued each year, to the non-charitable beneficiary. The NIMCRUT, however, provides that if the trust's income for the year is less than the specified distribution percentage, the non-charitable beneficiary (you) will receive only an amount equal to the actual annual income. The good news is that if the trust's income in future years exceeds the specified distribution amount, the trust will "make up" the shortfall in previous years' payments.

Advantages

There are several possible tax implications to be considered when utilizing a CRT. First, contributions to CRTs generally create some type of **charitable income tax deduction**. The deduction is computed using a formula that calculates the value of the gift that charity will receive in the future.

With most common contributions such as publicly traded securities, the deduction is based on the current fair market value of the assets on the date of the transfer. However, in some instances, the deduction may be based on the cost basis of the contributed property. Charitable income tax deductions can be utilized in the year of the contribution and for five succeeding years if the deduction is not fully used in year one. These deductions are subject to limitations depending on the property contributed and the nature of the ultimate charitable beneficiary.

CHAPTER 36   Charitable Annuity Trusts and Unitrusts

The **saving of capital gains tax** is another important aspect of planning with CRTs. When an appreciated long term gain asset is contributed to a CRT and then sold, the CRT does not immediately owe any income tax. Instead, the capital gain is "stored" in the trust. As the trust pays out distributions to the income beneficiary, a portion of the income may be taxed at the capital gains rates. Thus the capital gains may be deferred over a very long period allowing the principal of the trust to be fully invested and productive.

Lastly, in most common CRTs where a husband and wife are income beneficiaries, when the last of them dies, the assets of the CRT are out of the estate for **estate tax** purposes. (Note that if the CRT is a term-of-years trust instead of a lifetime trust, and the income beneficiary dies before the expiration of the term of years, then the values of the future income stream may still be included in the estate.)

> Charitable trusts are ways to provide for the kids, give to charity, and save taxes. The two most common types of charitable trusts are the Charitable Remainder Trust and the Charitable Lead Trust.

What about my heirs?

Since the principal of the CRT passes to charity at the end of the income term, the heirs are disinherited as to the CRT assets. If this is a concern, this problem may be remedied by establishing a separate wealth replacement trust. A wealth replacement trust is another name for the irrevocable life insurance trust (ILIT) mentioned in Chapter 18. By way of reminder, an ILIT is an irrevocable trust that purchases a life insurance policy on the life or lives of the CRT's income beneficiaries. The heirs are the beneficiaries of this new trust, and the life insurance replaces the CRT principal that passes to charity at the end of the CRT's income term.

Charitable Lead Annuity Trusts and Unitrusts (CLATs and CLUTs): The Charity Gets the Annual Payment, You or Your Beneficiary Get the Remainder

How They Work

A charitable lead trust (CLT) is an irrevocable trust which provides for distribution of annual payments to a charitable beneficiary or beneficiaries, with the remainder distributed to a non-charitable beneficiary or beneficiaries upon the death of the trustmaker, or upon expiration of a fixed period of time. It is sometimes thought of as the reverse of the charitable remainder trust.

Similar to charitable remainder trusts, there are two types of lead trusts: Charitable Lead Annuity Trusts (CLATs) and Charitable Lead Unitrusts (CLUTs).

A CLAT is established so that the payment to charity needs to be calculated only when the trust is established. Generally the payment remains level over the term of the trust and is independent of the performance of the underlying assets. A CLUT recalculates its distribution annually based on a fixed percentage of the assets in the trust. Depending on investment performance, the payment to charity may go up or down.

Advantages

First, the trustmaker transfers assets to the trust for a term of years. Assets could be cash, securities, fine art, or other property.

Next, annual payments are made from the trust to a designated charity or charities. Payments can be based on a fixed amount or a set percentage of the trust's value each year depending on how the trust is structured.

For tax purposes, the IRS uses a set rate to project the trust's growth. This determines the taxable gift that will pass to the heirs. If the trust grows beyond that amount, the gains or the appreciation passes to the heirs, estate tax free.

To totally avoid gift tax consequences on the assets passed to the heirs, investors can "zero out" the trust by structuring the annual charitable payments so that they equal the original value of the assets donated to the trust.

One of the most common applications of CLTs is a special trust that comes into play at the death of the grantor. Called a Testamentary Charitable Lead Annuity Trust (TCLAT), this trust is used to take any assets that remain in the estate above the current remaining estate tax exemption and to create a trust that is the right combination of term and payout so as to create a "zero" remainder interest. These trusts effectively can eliminate any remaining taxable estate and therefore any estate tax. The trade-off is that the heirs will have a considerable delay in receiving these assets.

There are specific rules for computing the estate or charitable deduction which are based on the value of the gift to charity over the term of the trust. Generally, with a longer trust term, and a higher payout rate, the larger the charitable deduction.

CHAPTER 37

Private Foundations

Only if you're leaving $1 million or more to charity, and have a person with a charitable passion as strong as your own

A private foundation is a special type of tax exempt entity that is most often established by a single family to fulfill its charitable mission. There are operating and non-operating foundations, though most private foundations are of the non-operating type.

Private foundations have very specific rules and regulations that must be strictly adhered to. Most well known is the rule that mandates a 5% distribution to charity annually. However, there are also rules against self-dealing, holding certain types of investments known as "jeopardy investments," and rules against creating excessive personal benefits from the foundation. While it is common to have family members on the Board of Directors get paid for their services, pay must be reasonable compared to other similar-sized charities.

Contributions to private foundations generally create an income tax charitable deduction, subject to the deductibility limitations. Deductions are available in the year of the gift and can be carried forward for five succeeding years if needed. Contributions may be deductible at fair market value or cost basis, depending on the type of asset contributed. Private foundations are tax-exempt under most circumstances but caution must be taken if assets that create Unrelated Business Taxable Income (UBTI) are being considered.

A family with a considerable collection of art or antiques or classic cars might consider using an operating foundation, essentially establishing their own "museum." While the collection may not be housed in a single physical facility, it would allow the family to keep the collection together, exhibit it around the world by loaning it to other museums, maintain it, and otherwise keep it within family control.

Advantages of a Private Foundation

A private foundation provides the donor more direct control over operations of the private foundation than a donor can exercise over a fund at a community foundation. The private foundation often provides a more prominent connection between the donor's family and philanthropy within the community. The private foundation can also pay reasonable compensation and expenses (including subsequent generations of involved family members), relating to the foundation's activities, from donated proceeds.

> Private foundations are appropriate only if you're leaving at least $1,000,000 to charity, and have a person with a charitable passion as strong as your own.

For most families, the establishment of a private foundation only makes sense if you're leaving at least $1 million to charity, and if you have family members who are as passionate as you are about the charitable causes the foundation supports. A less complex way to keep your family involved in philanthropy, without the complexities of a private foundation, is discussed in Chapter 38.

CHAPTER 38

Community Foundations and Donor Advised Funds

How to "borrow" a 501(c)(3) charitable organization with the same results at a much lower cost – and you can include family

A community foundation is an independent non-operating pubic charity working in a specific geographic area to manage a collection of charitable funds from various donors in the community. There are more than 700 community foundations nationwide; many dating back to the early 1900s. Collectively, community foundations manage more than $40 Billion in charitable assets and distribute millions of dollars to charitable organizations each year.

A community foundation is a vehicle for charitable giving, not an end user of charitable donations. Community foundations help people achieve their philanthropic dreams by accepting, managing, administering, and distributing charitable funds created by individuals and families. Gifts to the community foundation can take the form of donor-advised funds, endowments, gift annuities, charitable remainder trusts, and others.

The Donor-Advised Fund at a Community Foundation

A donor makes an irrevocable gift to a special fund established within the community foundation, which usually bears the donor's or the donor's family name. The donor receives an immediate income tax charitable deduction for the gift. The gift is invested and accumulated tax free by the community foundation,

CHAPTER 38   Community Foundations and Donor Advised Funds

similar to an endowment. The donor can request, at any time, that part or the entire fund be paid to a charity that the donor selects. The donor can select any number of charities in any proportion the donor chooses.

The community foundation makes all of the investment decisions and the donor advises the community foundation when and how much to pay out to charities selected by the donor. The community foundation is able to pool various charitable funds established by its donors for a greater market return, thus keeping overhead and expenses low, and maximizing the amounts being given to the charities selected by the donor from the donor's fund.

Advantages of the Community Foundation over a Private Foundation

There are many practical reasons why establishing a charitable fund at a community foundation might make more sense than creating a private foundation. Some of these reasons include:

- A fund at the community foundation is easy and inexpensive to establish, while a private foundation requires a donor to create a new organization, apply for tax-exempt status, pay filing fees, and incur legal and accounting expenses.

- The income tax charitable deduction limitation on a gift of cash to a community foundation is 50% of the adjusted gross income of the donor for the year of the gift, while that same gift to a private foundation is limited to 30% of the donor's adjusted gross income.

- The charitable deduction for a gift of appreciated stock to a private foundation is limited to its cost basis, up to 20% of the donor's adjusted gross income. That same gift to a community foundation may be deducted at its fair market value, up to 30% of the donor's adjusted gross income.

- A private foundation is required to pay an excise tax of 2% on its investment income and net realized capital gains, while a fund

CHAPTER 38   Community Foundations and Donor Advised Funds

at a community foundation does not, because the community foundation is a public charity.

- Gifts made to a community foundation can remain anonymous, while a private foundation is required to make available to the public the name and address of any substantial contributor.

- A private foundation must distribute at least 5% of its net investment assets to charities each year, regardless of whether the private foundation has earned any investment income that year. A charitable fund at a community foundation does not have any minimum annual distribution requirements, thus allowing the fund to grow from year to year at the discretion of the donor.

- A private foundation is subject to strict regulations on self-dealing between the foundation and those who manage, control, or contribute to it and persons or corporations closely related to them. There are fewer legal restrictions on a charitable fund at a community foundation.

> A community foundation is a charity you give "through," not "to."

- Community foundation funds have fewer investment restrictions than a private foundation. A private foundation, for example, may not hold more than 20% ownership in a particular corporation.

- There are fewer IRS reporting requirements on community foundation grants and funds than those on private foundations. Any reporting requirements are part of the community foundation's annual reporting to the IRS, and include all of the community foundation funds and grants at no additional charge to the funds the community foundation administers.

CHAPTER 39

Charitable Annuities

If you are giving to the "Big Boys" it can make a lot of sense

As mentioned earlier, one of the disadvantages of direct gifts is that it will impact your current net worth and income to live on. One way to offset the income disadvantage is to make a gift as part of a "charitable gift annuity." In exchange for your gift, the charity commits to pay a specified amount each year for the rest of your life. You get a tax deduction for the amount of the contribution that exceeds the value of the annuity.

A charitable gift annuity is a way to make a gift to your favorite charity, and still receive an income for yourself or others. It is a contract under which a charity, in return for a transfer of cash or other property, agrees to pay a fixed sum of money for a period measured by one or two lives. The person who contributes an asset for the annuity is called the "donor," and the person who receives payments is called the "annuitant" or "beneficiary." Usually, the annuitant is also the donor, but this is not always true. The maximum number of annuitants is two, and payments can be made to them jointly or successively.

> **A charitable gift annuity is a way to make a gift to your favorite charity, and still receive an income for yourself or others.**

The policies for gift annuities will vary from charity to charity, so be sure to do thorough research and due diligence.

CHAPTER 39   Charitable Annuities

A commercial annuity, by comparison, may allow more than you and your spouse to be beneficiaries, and may continue payments to your beneficiaries for a period of years after your death. With a charitable gift annuity, the payments end with your death, or after the death of the second spouse. On the other hand, you won't get the charitable deductions with a commercial annuity that you get with the charitable annuity.

One of the things to consider, however, is that your payments depend on the financial strength of the charity. That's why it is not typically recommended that you enter into a charitable gift annuity with a new, small charity with few financial resources. The payments are guaranteed by the charity, and all its assets are available to satisfy the payments. But if the charity goes out of business, you'll lose your income with little recourse.

CHAPTER 40

Business Succession Planning

You need to have a plan if you want your business to continue when you're disabled or deceased

The Importance of Business Succession Planning

If you own a business, it's critical that you and your professional advisory team design a comprehensive plan; from the starting point of choosing the type of business entity, to the eventual exit strategy and plan for business succession.

The track record of family businesses enduring longer than the first or second generation is abysmal. Ironically, companies pour a lot of money into marketing, research and development, information technology, and employees, but fail to plan for the succession and long-term success of the company.

If you have a strong succession plan in place, and communicate that plan to the senior executives or management team while you are alive and well, that will allow you to explain your decisions to your successors, and begin to train them to take over.

If you die without a comprehensive succession plan, your interest in the company will be included among all of your other assets. The company will pass to the beneficiaries named in your will or trust – regardless of whether or not they have any involvement or interest in the business.

CHAPTER 40   Business Succession Planning

For example, all of your assets might be divided equally among three children: one who has worked in your company and two who haven't. As a result, the child most likely to keep the company going will lack the necessary control and motivation to continue to grow the company for the benefit of people not working in the business. Such inequities can create serious family conflict and potentially a total loss of the business.

Also, for many business owners, the business is the primary asset they own – with few additional liquid assets. If the business is dependent primarily upon your efforts, and you become disabled or die without a plan in place, the business is likely to fail. All of its value is therefore lost to your spouse and children.

Another problem is that you could face significant estate taxes depending on the value of your company, and the estate tax exemption and tax rates in effect at death. Federal estate tax rates over the years have been as high as 60% and as low as 35% and exemptions have ranged from $600,000 to more than $5 million. State inheritance tax might also be due. If you die with a company worth $10 million and also have $2 million of other assets, the total federal estate tax bill at a $1 million exemption could be more than $6,000,000! If the federal estate tax exemption is $5 million, your federal estate tax liability could still be as high as $4,000,000.

If your estate includes only $2 million outside of the business, where will the money come from to pay those taxes which are due within 9 months of your death? Your heirs could be forced to borrow heavily to pay the estate tax. Or they might have to sell the company even though you planned to keep it in the family. If others know that you are liquidating under a deadline, it could cause the business to be sold at a drastic discount.

With proper planning, all of these problems can be avoided, and taxes can be minimized. You can be sure that your company will pass into good hands, that the full value of the company will be realized if it's sold, that you can reduce the future estate tax bill, all while nurturing strong and lasting family relationships.

CHAPTER 40   Business Succession Planning

Planning for Family Members not Involved in the Business

When only one child or fewer than all the children work in the family business, careful planning is required. Many of our business owner clients seek advice on how to handle such a situation "fairly."

In most cases the business owner wants to ensure that the business interests will pass to the child or children actively involved in the business. Some transfers may be accomplished during the parents' lifetimes, while in other cases the parents will prefer to pass the interests only upon their deaths.

There are many questions to consider when planning the transfer of a closely-held business to family members. First, are the members of the family currently employed in the business capable or interested in continuing the business after the owner's death? Is the surviving spouse working in the business? If not, how will she draw income from the business if not employed?

If there is no family heir capable or interested in the business, is there a non-family executive, manager, or group of employees who might be interested in buying the business? Will the non-family employees stay with the company after the owner dies? Will customers transfer their business to a competitor? If the business had to be liquidated, what value would it bring? What value might the IRS put on the business for estate tax purposes?

> You need a plan if you want your business to continue when you're disabled or deceased. The track record of family and small businesses enduring longer than the first or second generation is abysmal.

If you intend to equalize the inheritance between the children, it is very important to obtain a qualified valuation to determine what your business is really worth. Only then can you determine whether you have enough "other" assets that will permit you to leave the business assets to the "business" children, with some or all of the remaining assets to the "non-business" children.

CHAPTER 40   Business Succession Planning

In cases where the value of the business is significantly greater than the non-business assets, life insurance may be the great equalizer. If you are insurable, you can obtain sufficient life insurance (preferably owned in an ILIT) that will leave the death benefit to the non-active children, with the business assets of equivalent value passing to the active children.

But what if you're uninsurable or you cannot afford enough insurance to equalize the value of the business and non-business assets? In such cases, you might consider including in your business operating documents a provision that affords the active children the right to buy out the interests of the non-active children in the business for that portion of the business value that exceeds the value of any life insurance or non-business assets.

If insurance is unavailable or insufficient, then you might stipulate that the buyout would be made in installment payments memorialized by a promissory note, typically secured by business assets, or by the business entity interests being purchased.

CHAPTER 41

Buy-Sell Agreements

If you are in business with someone else, and the business is important to you or your family, you need one

Introduction to Buy-Sell Agreements

Buy-Sell agreements let owners or shareholders of a corporation agree to the terms and conditions of a future sale to ease the transfer of ownership under certain triggering events. A triggering event might include a partner's death, retirement, termination of employment, loss of a professional license, disability, divorce (or transfer of ownership to a spouse), bankruptcy, insolvency, or receipt of a third-party offer to purchase the business.

Some of the benefits of a buy-sell agreement include:

- It gives an owner a ready market for his or her business interest.
- It resolves estate liquidity issues.
- It provides a framework for establishing the purchase price.
- It reduces disputes.

A typical buy-sell agreement will specify the type of agreement, the triggers that will cause a mandatory or optional buyout, a determination of the appropriate valuation date imposed by the agreement, the payment terms of the buy-sell obligation, the methods by which the agreement will be funded, non-compete agreements between the parties, and which transfers of interests are permitted or prohibited by the agreement. Buy-sell agreements can be used with any type of business.

Types of Buy-Sell Agreements

There are three types of buy-sell agreements: cross-purchase, redemption, and hybrid. They can be summarized as follows:

Cross-Purchase Agreements – Upon an owner's demise the remaining owners individually agree to redeem the business interest of the deceased. The most common way partners prepare for funding a purchase in the event of death or disability is to have each owner obtain life or disability insurance policies on the other partners in amounts sufficient to pay for the business interest.

- Advantages – The surviving partners in a cross-purchase agreement typically receive any life insurance proceeds tax-free. Those proceeds are not includible in the decedent's estate. The agreement's definition of fair market value for the business may or may not be acceptable to the IRS for estate tax purposes. But if it is, the estate or its beneficiaries will have no tax on the purchase of the owner's interest because the basis of the interest will be equal to its sale price.

- Disadvantages – Purchasing a life or disability insurance policy on the life of each of the other partners becomes increasingly complex to administer as the number of owners changes over time. The cost of the insurance may be disproportionate if the owners are of different ages and states of health. If there is no insurance, the funding will come from the after-tax income of the remaining owners. If a surviving owner must borrow the funds for the buyout, the IRS may classify the interest paid on the loan as investment interest, delaying the deductibility of the amounts paid.

Redemption Buy-Sell Agreements – Upon a triggering event, the business entity itself typically redeems the interest of the departing owner. The buyout may be funded by the immediate use of the business's resources, a financing arrangement defined by the agreement, the remaining owners' personal savings, or life or disability insurance on the life of the departing owner.

> If you are in business with someone else, and the business is important to you or your family, you need a buy-sell agreement.

- Advantages – The business is responsible for funding the agreement. The agreement may define the fair market value of the decedent's interest for estate tax purposes. If so, the estate or its beneficiaries will have no tax on the purchase of the decedent's interest. If the agreement isn't fully funded and surviving owners borrow to fund the buyout, interest payments to the estate will be deductible on the entity's tax return.

- Disadvantages – If a corporate entity is the beneficiary of insurance used for the buyout, the proceeds of the policy may be subject to the alternative minimum tax. And if the corporation establishes a savings account in anticipation of the buyout, that could create accumulated earnings tax problems.

The Hybrid Buy-Sell Agreement – This type of agreement is also called a "combination" or a "wait and see" agreement. It typically gives the issuing business the first right of refusal to buy the ownership interest of the departing owner, and other owners the second option to buy.

Conclusion

Depending on the nature and ownership of the business entity, types of agreements and triggers will vary, but every effective agreement should anticipate the need for funding and provide a procedure to determine the purchase price. It is also important that the agreement be kept up to date with changes in the business entity. Improperly structured buy-sell agreements can produce unintended tax results. Business owners should use a competent team of planning professionals including their business and estate planning attorney(s), their CPA, and their financial advisor.

CHAPTER 42

Planning for Same Sex and Unwed Couples

Planning for couples who are "unmarried" is not the same as planning for two people who are "single"

The Need

More and more couples are choosing to remain unwed. Many advisors confuse "unwed" with "single" and thus do not adequately plan for same sex and unwed couples ("partners"). There are several reasons why couples remain unwed. Perhaps they are apprehensive from previous divorces. Or perhaps it's because marriage is not permitted for same sex relationships. Sometimes it's the "marriage penalty" imposed by the IRS on income taxes for higher income couples.

Civil Union is not the same as marriage under the law, so unwed couples are excluded from several benefits:

- Federal benefits under the Social Security rules for survivors

- Insurance benefits through a partner's employer

- Receiving wages, workers' compensation, and retirement plan benefits for a deceased partner

- Filing joint income tax returns

CHAPTER 42   Planning for Same Sex and Unwed Couples

- Creating a "family partnership" under federal tax laws which allows you to divide business income among family members

- Spousal inheritance protections under probate law

- Spousal priority preferences for health care and disability proxies

- Transfer of assets with no gift and estate taxes

- Alimony and other rights upon dissolution of relationship

Particular Challenges Related to Estate Planning

Besides the exclusions listed above, there are some specific challenges that must be addressed when undertaking estate planning for same sex or unwed couples.

Homestead Protection – Same sex partners are not considered "surviving spouses" or "lineal descendants" in most states. Thus the homestead creditor protections available to spouses are not available to non-spouse partners.

Intestacy Laws – The worst case scenario is for two partners to have no estate planning at all. When someone passes away without an estate plan, they are said to be intestate, and state law will determine what happens to their assets. When there are spouses and descendants, the laws of most states are fairly clear as to who gets what. If no spouse or descendants, the law usually passes the assets to the deceased's parents, if living, or to siblings. If none of them are living, the assets may go to more distant relatives. If no relatives are found the assets are said to "escheat" to the state – meaning that the state will dispose of the funds as dictated by statute – sometimes to schools or other beneficiaries. Note that intestacy laws do NOT include non-married partners.

No Unlimited Marital Deduction – The unlimited marital deduction allows assets to be passed to a surviving spouse without estate taxes – regardless of the size of the estate. The deduction does not exist for non-married partners, and this can cause unintended problems and pitfalls when one partner passes away – especially if there is a disparity in wealth between the two. If the

CHAPTER 42   Planning for Same Sex and Unwed Couples

wealthier partner dies first, estate taxes could take a large percentage of the assets, leaving far less for the survivor.

Powers of Attorney – In the event of disability, when there is no valid Power of Attorney for Health Care, the incapacitated person's next of kin would be given authority to make health care decisions. In the case of unmarried partners, authority would be given first to the incapacitated partner's adult children, then to parents, siblings, or other blood relatives. This scenario can be problematic if the next of kin cannot be found; is out of state or unreachable; is not aware of the incapacitated person's wishes; or they do not approve of the unwed couple's partner or lifestyle. If next of kin cannot be located, the court will issue an emergency guardianship order until a permanent guardian can be found.

> Planning for couples who are "unmarried" is not the same as planning for two people who are "single."

Planning Strategies

There are several strategies that can be implemented to help alleviate some of the challenges of planning for unwed and same sex couples. The most important thing, of course, is having an up-to-date estate plan.

Irrevocable Life Insurance Trusts – Life insurance can play an important role in many situations. It can be used to provide for the surviving partner and ensure that he or she is not left with debts from the deceased partner. If the insurance is held in an Irrevocable Life Insurance Trust (ILIT) it is not includable in the deceased partner's estate, and since life insurance is not income taxable to beneficiaries, the proceeds of the policy can pass free of both income and estate taxes. Policies can be taken out on one or both partners' lives.

Jointly Titled and Transfer on Death (T.O.D.) Accounts – Accounts that are titled jointly or have a T.O.D. designation will pass automatically to the surviving partner. Although a T.O.D. designation is generally less complicated than joint ownership, it is a foolish choice except for minimal amounts, because of the lack of asset protection. In addition, if an unmarried couple titles assets jointly there are gift tax considerations; there could be estate taxes on the second death; and the partners must discuss what would happen in the event of a break-up.

CHAPTER 42   Planning for Same Sex and Unwed Couples

Cohabitation Agreements – A cohabitation agreement is a contract that typically covers such things as financial support obligations during the relationship or upon its dissolution; handling payment of debts; distributing property and dividing the principal residence in case of death or breakup; specifying health insurance coverage and decisions about emergency medical decisions; determining the right to serve as guardian or conservator in the event of incapacitation; and defining support, custody, or visitation rights for minor children (although nonbinding) or pets.

Regardless of how close your relationship is with your partner, living together does not automatically entitle either one of you to the rights and protections afforded to married couples. It is therefore important for you and your partner to state your rights and obligations in a legal document in the event of a breakup or death. A cohabitation agreement will ensure that you and your partner are protected at the same time that it clarifies your understanding of the relationship.

CHAPTER 43

Special Needs Trusts

Don't jump too quickly because this may not be right for your situation

Some of our clients have children or grandchildren with special needs or disabilities, thus presenting special challenges in their planning. The special needs heir may be supported by Social Security disability income, Supplemental Security Income, or Medicaid benefits. Although our clients want to include the special needs person in their estate plan, they are concerned that an inheritance of any type will make the child or grandchild ineligible for the programs upon which they depend. So they worry that they'll have to disinherit that special needs person.

Fortunately, there is a way to include special needs heirs in your estate plan – it's called a Special Needs Trust (SNT). These trusts can be established during life, but most clients make it part of their plan to take effect after they pass away.

How It Works

You set up a trust that names the special needs person as the beneficiary, and gives the trustee of the trust the right to make distributions on behalf of the special needs person. The trustee is instructed to not make any distributions that will threaten the government support being received by the beneficiary. The trust may also include specific suggestions (not requirements) on how the trustee might use the assets of the trust to help the special needs beneficiary, or

CHAPTER 43   Special Needs Trusts

those suggestions could be put into a separate Memorandum of Wishes that is referenced in the trust.

For example, if you know it makes the special needs person happy to have their hair done, you could suggest that the Trustee make funds available every few weeks for a trip to the hair salon. Or maybe the beneficiary loves movies, so the Trustee may elect to distribute funds to Best Buy for a DVD player and a wide assortment of movies – or pay for a weekly trip to the theater. These are the types of needs that will enhance the happiness of the special needs person, and improve their life – but that may not be covered by the government support programs. Your inheritance can be used in this way to give them a better quality of life.

Choosing a Trustee

The key to a successful special needs trust is that it is managed by a trustee who makes direct payments for products and services on behalf of the special needs person, without money going directly to the special needs person.

The trustee of the SNT is given great discretion when it comes to distributions from the trust, which makes the trustee very important and very powerful. Therefore, care should be taken when choosing a trustee. Many clients would prefer to name a friend or family member, but there are several challenges with that choice. Does the family member have the time and skill to invest the trust assets successfully? Are they able to file tax returns, keep accurate records, and keep up with Social Security and Medicaid rules? And of course, you can never be sure that any person will outlive the special needs person.

> Don't jump too quickly, because this may not be right for your situation.

The alternative is to hire a corporate trustee like a bank or trust company. The obvious problem with that approach is that the corporate trustee may never even meet the special needs person, and certainly doesn't have a personal relationship with them – or a personal concern with their well-being. It's "just business" for the corporate trustee, and as a business, they will, of course, charge a fee for their services.

To balance the business approach of the trustee, you could appoint an Advisory Panel made up of family members or others, to watch out for the welfare of the special needs person from a personal perspective. You can also authorize the trustee to hire a "personal care manager" who will check up on the beneficiary to ensure their needs are being met. You can also appoint a "trust protector" who is authorized to make administrative changes to the trust if the legal rules change.

Not the Solution for Every Special Needs Situation

You would be wise to carefully consider before jumping into a special needs trust. They can certainly be created if that ends up being the best solution, but remember that the trust will require careful design and implementation, and there may be other solutions.

For example, if your estate is large enough, your special needs beneficiary may not even need government benefits. Your inheritance could replace those benefits, and provide a better lifestyle without limitations. Instead of passing the assets themselves, you could also use some of those assets to buy an insurance policy (within an Irrevocable Life Insurance Trust) for the benefit of the special needs person. Of course, you'll still need a reliable trustee or advisory panel to take care of the beneficiary if they are unable to care for themselves or make their own financial decisions.

CHAPTER 44

Long Term Care Insurance

Is it right for you – or do you have sufficient assets to self-insure

Most of our clients have enough wealth that they'll never have to worry about going to Medicaid for help to pay nursing home costs, and they don't even need long-term care insurance. They can easily pay for whatever develops in their health or their life. Many people, however, would be encouraged to at least consider long-term care insurance.

A long-term care policy can be quite affordable, especially if you purchase it before age 50. The purpose of the policy is to cover the costs of your eventual disability and long-term care. Some of the things to consider when you shop for a policy include:

1. Does the type of policy I'm considering shift the risk from me to the insurance company?

2. Is the policy good for my entire lifetime?

3. Does it pay 100% of the benefits for home care as well as care in an institution?

4. If you are under age 75 and buying a lifetime policy, does the policy have an "inflation rider" that increases the benefit to match the rate of inflation?

Some of these features will add to the cost of the policy, so that has to be weighed when choosing policy types and specific features. One "rule of thumb" that has been used by some advisors is that if the annual premium for a policy with these features is less than 15% of the projected income from retirement assets, it is probably worthwhile.

> Is it right for you? Or do you have sufficient assets to self-insure?

If a person has long-term care needs and is uninsured they will typically still receive the care they need. They will either be able to pay for that care or will spend down their assets and be able to qualify for Medicaid.

What often goes overlooked, however, is the situation of the non-disabled spouse still living in the community. Not only does the well spouse often have the difficult task of caring for the disabled spouse, but if assets are depleted until the disabled spouse qualifies for Medicaid, the well spouse may be left with very little to live on for the rest of his or her life.

When considering long-term care insurance, remember to consider not only the cost of the care itself, but the costs to the non-disabled spouse if there is no insurance to pay for that care. When the first spouse passes away the well spouse may still be left with many years of health, and no assets with which to enjoy them.

The decision about long-term care insurance should be carefully considered with your insurance professional and the rest of your advisory team.

CHAPTER 45

Elder Law

Navigating confusing waters for people with challenging needs

Elder law is actually a very broad area of law that mainly focuses on the legal needs of the elderly and planning for individuals with special needs. These needs often include traditional financial, insurance, and estate planning. But elder law also encapsulates planning for state Medicaid benefits in a long-term health care setting, and even incidents of financial or physical elder abuse. In our practice, the most common discussions in elder law are about Medicaid planning and Special Needs Trusts. Medicaid planning will be the focus of this chapter.

Medicaid planning encompasses an array of different techniques that are designed to help preserve your assets in the event you or your spouse require long-term health care as a result of failing health or disability, whether mental or physical. Many people who have significant health problems require round-the-clock assistance. The costs for such custodial care – which in a nursing home setting can be over $15,000 per month in some states – are generally your financial responsibility in the absence of careful and intentional planning.

Medicare (different than Medicaid) provides only limited coverage for those persons who require such "custodial" care. Some people will have the foresight to purchase long-term care insurance to cover most if not all of these costs. But the vast majority of Americans do not purchase long-term care insurance, leaving only two primary sources to cover the long-term care expenses: personal assets or the Medicaid program.

CHAPTER 45   Elder Law

Medicaid is designed as a "safety net" to provide health care coverage for those with more limited assets and income. It is actually a type of "welfare" benefit. Under current law, a person can qualify for Medicaid coverage for long-term care costs only after their assets (typically excluding a primary residence and certain other assets, depending on state law) have been reduced to a very low amount – in some states as little as $2,000, up to a maximum in other states of perhaps $15,000. Most people who have significant long-term care requirements end up "spending down" virtually all of their assets until they achieve Medicaid eligibility. That, of course, leaves nothing to pass on to your children and other loved ones, and even more importantly, can leave the non-disabled spouse destitute.

Medicaid planning often entails exploring ways that families can keep from wiping out all their assets before qualifying for benefits. There are really two types of planning: proactive planning that is designed and implemented well in advance of any long-term health care needs; and crisis planning that is put in place at the time you require long-term care. In almost every circumstance, engaging in proactive planning will preserve more of your assets.

Generally speaking, you must be mostly impoverished to be eligible for Medicaid benefits. One way to become impoverished is to spend all of your assets for that long-term medical care. All "countable" assets will have to be "spent down" by paying personally for your custodial care.

Another way to become impoverished is to give all your assets away to the people who would eventually inherit them, before they are all spent on those medical costs. The only problem is that if you give away those assets within five years of entering the long-term care facility, you will still have to pay approximately the equivalent value of those assets for your care, before you can take advantage of the Medicaid program.

Proactive Medicaid planning techniques are based on a fundamental concept: effectively transferring your assets in a manner that will either cause otherwise "countable" assets to be "non-countable" or that will "trigger" the start of the current five-year "look-back" period so that when and if you need long-term care, the transferred assets will no longer be part of your "countable" assets subject to a Medicaid "spend down." The good news is that some planning techniques may allow you to transfer assets in a manner that will still provide you with a degree of access and control.

To help protect your assets in the event of a potential long-term health care crisis, you might consider including as part of your overall estate plan, an irrevocable trust that, for the sake of this discussion, we'll call a "Medicaid Trust." A Medicaid Trust is a particular type of irrevocable trust, used because revocable trusts are not effective asset protection vehicles. As discussed in earlier chapters, since the Trustmaker of a revocable trust has access to the assets, under Medicaid rules the assets are deemed "available" to the Trustmaker and must be "spent down" before the Trustmaker becomes eligible for Medicaid coverage.

However, assets that are transferred to a properly structured Medicaid Trust will be deemed transferred as of the date the assets are titled in the name of the Trust. This transfer will "start the clock running" on the five-year Medicaid "look-back" period.

> It is vital to plan earlier rather than later.

Medicaid law is state-specific so each case must be considered independently. If this type of planning is a concern for you, we will discuss your options as part of a comprehensive estate planning consultation.

CHAPTER 46

The Inheriting Trust

How to talk to Mom and Dad about their estate plan

Estate planning is one of the most difficult things for most adults to discuss with their aging parents. And yet, it's important to do so. Everyone knows that it saves time, money, and grief to have your affairs in order before you pass away. In fact, most parents have been teaching their children to "plan ahead" since they were in grade school.

But when it comes to estate planning, there seems to be a superstition among some seniors that by completing their plan, it will speed their death. Some adult children believe that if they bring up the topic, their parents will think they are greedy and "just waiting for them to die so they can get an inheritance." On the other hand, some adult children do not wish to get involved in detailed discussions of financial affairs – because that's "just not done" in their family.

You have learned about the advantages of leaving an inheritance in trust where it is protected from creditors and predators, and would like your parents to pass things to you with those protections. And even though you simply want some direction about what to do in the event of their death or disability, neither side wants to talk about it. We'd like to suggest a solution.

The "Inheriting Trust" is a great way to open this tough discussion with your parents, and it can help to painlessly transition the conversation to other topics that are tough to bring up, but are important to talk about.

CHAPTER 46 The Inheriting Trust

> "The Inheriting Trust is an irrevocable trust that you, the adult child, establish now. It is designed to receive an inheritance that would otherwise have been passed outright to you – without any protections."

An Inheriting Trust is an irrevocable trust that you, the adult child, establish now. It is a special type of dynasty trust that is designed to receive an inheritance that would otherwise have been passed outright to you – and without protections. It provides the inheritor with all the rights, benefits, and control he or she would have through outright ownership, along with tax, creditor, and divorce protections that would not be available in an outright distribution.

The inheritor is either the sole trustee, or a co-trustee who has the ability to remove and replace the other co-trustee and select a successor. The purpose of the trust is to serve as a receptacle for any inheritance you might receive from your parents or others. It can be initially funded with as little as ten dollars until such time as the inheritance is received.

If your parents are making use of a gifting program to reduce the size of their estate, the Inheriting Trust also makes a good protected receptacle for those gifts.

Then, without having to ask about financial details, or discuss unpleasant topics, you can simply mention to your parents that you have established the trust, and explain to them how it works. You could say something like this:

> "Mom and Dad, we've been doing some estate planning for our family, and that reminded me of a couple of things. First, you know that I love you and I hope you live forever. And I also hope that you've been doing some planning too. Our planning is giving us great peace of mind, and I think you'll experience the same thing.
>
> "Also, I wanted you to know that we've set up trusts for our kids so that if anything of value is left when we pass away, it will go to our kids in a way that nobody else can touch it. It will be safe from divorces, lawsuits, and all the bad things that can happen in life.

CHAPTER 46   The Inheriting Trust

"Since we weren't sure if you have had the chance to do any planning, we also went ahead and set up a special trust that is intended to protect any inheritance that we might receive someday. So when you're thinking about those things that you want to leave to your kids someday, we'd prefer that you leave things to that trust we've set up, instead of directly to us. That way, if something bad is happening in our lives at that moment, the inheritance you leave behind can't be taken from us."

Consider an Inheriting Trust to provide peace of mind for both you and your parents!

CHAPTER 47

Estate Settlement

Even with a trust there are things that need to be done after you're gone
(but nowhere near as bad as probate)

We earlier talked about some of the disadvantages of probate, and how it can be avoided through trust-centered planning. However, avoiding probate does not mean that there is nothing at all to do after you're gone. The person responsible for settling an estate is called the executor in some states or, more often, the Personal Representative (PR). The person responsible for settling a trust is the successor trustee (Trustee). In the list below, we'll assume that the decedent used a fully funded trust plan, so the Trustee is taking primary responsibility for settlement, without the need for probate.

Here are the typical steps involved in estate and trust settlement. Note that some of the details and the order of events may vary from state to state:

1. The Decedent's will (pour-over will in a trust plan) is located and filed with the court in the county where the decedent resided at the time of death.

2. The Trustee locates and takes possession of the Decedent's records.

3. The Trustee takes measures to protect the Decedent's personal effects and other property (for example, making sure the house

CHAPTER 47   Estate Settlement

is secure and that no one is driving the Decedent's car or removing items of personal property).

4. Death notices and notices of estate administration are sent out to all the beneficiaries, as well as to reasonably ascertainable creditors of the Decedent.

5. The Trustee obtains a taxpayer ID for the Decedent's trust, and notifies financial institutions that he or she is the successor trustee of the financial accounts.

6. If assets are located outside the state of death, the Trustee must determine how these assets are to be handled, and what outside advisors might be required.

7. The Trustee redirects the Decedent's mail.

8. The Trustee should determine if the Decedent was due any unpaid salary or bonuses from his or her employment, or any death benefits from Social Security or the Department of Veterans' Affairs.

9. The Trustee obtains information on all assets owned by the Decedent including those in the Decedent's own name, held jointly with others, held in trust, life insurance proceeds, retirement accounts, business interests, etc.

10. If the Decedent had an ongoing business, the Trustee determines what to do with the business (shut it down or sell it), and orders appraisals of the business assets as well as of real property and personal effects. It will be important that the Trustee is aware of any existing buy-sell agreements.

> Even with a trust there are things that need to be done after you're gone.

11. An inventory of the Decedent's assets is filed, although in some states, the inventory can be waived by consent of the beneficiaries.

CHAPTER 47 Estate Settlement

12. The Trustee determines (usually with the help of a CPA) if Federal and State estate tax returns will be necessary. If required, the Federal tax return (Form 706) must be filed within 9 months of the date of death.

13. If tax is due, the Trustee determines how it will be paid.

14. The Trustee investigates all claims filed against the estate to determine their validity.

15. The Trustee files the Decedent's final income tax return, and any fiduciary returns required for the trust.

16. Accountings are filed with the court and with the beneficiaries when required. If the administration is complex and expected to continue more than one year, the Trustee should consider filing interim accountings to keep the beneficiaries apprised of the status.

17. A final accounting is filed where required. Some states allow accounting to be waived by the beneficiaries, and some states allow the Trustee to file a statement in lieu of final accounting if approved by the beneficiaries.

18. Some states require a final Petition for Discharge.

19. The Trustee makes final distributions of the Decedent's property and obtains receipts from the beneficiaries.

Obviously, if you choose a family member as your successor Trustee, there are many things on this list which will be totally new to him or her. Typically the Trustee works closely with your legal and accounting advisors to settle the trust and estate, but you should certainly make them aware of these responsibilities ahead of time. Occasionally we offer workshops for successor trustees. Feel free to check with our office about future training opportunities.

CHAPTER 48

Avoiding Estate Litigation: Death, Greed, and Money

The lawyers win and the children hate each other

The last thing you want to happen after your death is that your children and loved ones become embroiled in a lawsuit, fighting over your estate. Strange things happen (or perhaps we should say people act strangely) when money is at stake. But litigation should be avoided at all costs. It tends to become a defining moment in a family – something that divides families for generations to come. The costs of litigation have been known to wipe out entire estates so that no one receives anything, except the lawyers of course.

The best way to avoid litigation is to go through a program of comprehensive estate and financial planning, making your wishes crystal clear, and putting into place the legal tools necessary to enforce your wishes. But even with the best plan, you can't guarantee that litigation will not occur. People can sue anyone for anything at any time – and you never know when a disgruntled ex-spouse or distant relative will appear to file a claim against an estate.

If that happens, an estate litigation attorney should be retained to represent the beneficiaries, Trustees, and personal representatives in various jurisdictions dealing with estate litigation and probate litigation matters.

A will contest challenges the admission of a will to probate or seeks to revoke the probate of a will that is already pending before the probate court. Because

CHAPTER 48 Avoiding Estate Litigation: Death, Greed, and Money

a trust is not part of the public record in the same way that a will is, it is usually tougher to contest the terms of a trust. But it's not impossible. The most common causes of action in both will contests and estate litigation include the following:

1. LACK OF CAPACITY – Under the law, a testator is required to have mental competency to make a last will and testament or trust and to understand the nature of his or her estate assets and the people to whom the estate assets are going to be distributed. A will or trust can be declared void if lack of capacity can be proven. Usually, incompetence is established through a prior medical diagnosis of dementia, senility, Alzheimer's or psychosis.

> PLANNING SOLUTION – In our firm, planning is completed only for clients who are mentally competent. If there is any doubt about their condition, a medical examination is required to ensure the plan's validity. This has prevented many cases from going to litigation.

2. UNDUE INFLUENCE – When the testator is compelled or coerced to execute a will or trust by a relative, friend, trusted advisor, or health care worker, that is called undue influence. In many cases, the undue "influencer" will upset a long-established estate plan where the bulk of the estate was to pass to the descendants or close relatives of the decedent. In other cases, one child of the decedent will coerce the parent to write the other children out of the will or trust.

The lawyers win, and the children hate each other!

> PLANNING SOLUTION – Our plans are completed only through direct consultation with our clients – not clients' children, siblings, friends, or others. We meet confidentially with the clients, and typically without other family members present. If a client wishes to have a family member attend the planning sessions, we will of course welcome them. But we will use additional caution to ensure that family members not in attendance are also being considered, and that the attending family member is there for moral support, not to make planning decisions for their parent.

3. LACK OF FORMALITIES – In most states, proper execution of a last will and testament or trust requires that the will or trust is signed by the testator and witnessed and signed by two unrelated parties. A last will and testament can be contested on the basis that it was not properly drafted, signed, or witnessed in accordance with the law.

> PLANNING SOLUTION – We go through a standardized process that ensures that every document is executed flawlessly including client signatures, witnesses, notaries, and other formalities as required by the particular states in which we practice.

4. BREACH OF FIDUCIARY DUTY – The personal representative of an estate or the Trustee of a trust owes the beneficiaries of the estate or trust certain fiduciary duties of honesty, prudence, and loyalty. When those duties are violated by a trustee or personal representative, a cause of action arises.

> PLANNING SOLUTION – Our documents are written in plain English as much as possible, rather than in legalese. We want to be sure that the client, the trustees, the beneficiaries, and others who read the document can easily understand and follow the directions of the trustmaker. Plus, we include provisions for replacement of trustees who are violating their duties, and ask our clients to name successor trustees ahead of time in case someone has to be replaced.

5. ELECTIVE SHARE – Some states provide an elective share to surviving spouses, which provides the surviving spouse with a portion of the deceased spouse's estate according to a statutory formula. Deadlines may be associated to make the elective share.

> PLANNING SOLUTION – We discuss the elective share rules with our clients for each of the states in which we practice. We ensure that the issue is discussed and resolved ahead of time, not after someone has passed away.

6. FORGED DOCUMENTS – If someone suspects that estate planning documents such as a will or a trust are forged, or that signatures have been forged, there will definitely be a legal challenge to the plan.

> PLANNING SOLUTION – We avoid this problem by following all the required formalities including witnesses and notaries (where required) to ensure that the signatures on our planning documents are provably valid.

CHAPTER 49

What Type of Estate Plan is Right for You?

The "cookie cutter" approach doesn't work

Every family is unique. There is no such thing as "one size fits all" when it comes to estate planning.

Foundational Planning

Every client needs foundational planning that includes a revocable living trust, pour-over will, financial power of attorney, health care surrogate, living will, quitclaim bill of sale, and a funding plan. It also includes state-of-the-art asset protection for the surviving spouse and children. In addition, foundational planning may include basic generation-skipping transfer tax planning to avoid a degree of estate tax in subsequent generations, and an IRA inheritance trust to provide asset protection and achieve other goals as the client passes retirement plan assets to beneficiaries.

Advanced Planning

Once the foundational elements of the plan are in place, advanced planning focuses on specific solutions to our client's objectives, challenges, and planning issues. As such, it is an integrated approach that provides planning choices to meet client goals. Advanced planning often incorporates sophisticated techniques including Irrevocable Life Insurance Trusts (ILITs), Qualified Personal Residence Trusts (QPRTs), Buildup Equity Retirement Trusts (BERTs), advanced generation-skipping transfer tax planning, Charitable Remainder Trusts (CRTs), Special Needs Trusts (SNTs), Limited Liability Companies (LLCs), Family Limited Partnerships (FLPs), Legacy Trusts, and much more. This list is not meant to be exhaustive, but rather illustrative of some of the tools that may be employed at this level.

Global Planning

Global planning requires personal and financial analysis which leads to a custom financial design for each client. This cash flow analysis and modeling is designed to ensure that both the immediate and long-term consequences of global planning meet the client's needs and goals. It is used most often by especially affluent families. There are no time-frame limitations placed on global planning as it is anticipated that the client/firm relationship and the planning will continue for the long term as the plan is implemented and maintained to achieve client goals.

For a client to be willing to engage in global planning, they must be comfortable with a long-term relationship, willing to engage the legal services to implement it, and prepared to tolerate some additional and necessary complexity. Global planning is about bringing an extraordinary level of value and service to the client and their estate planning.

The type of estate plan that is right for you can only be determined after careful and thorough discussions with your professional advisors. They need to consider much more than your financial statement. They need to understand your family situation, the challenges your kids and grandkids might be facing, your desire to leave a legacy, your tax situation, and many other factors that will apply only to your family and circumstances.

> The "cookie cutter" approach to planning doesn't work.

CHAPTER 50

The Cost of Estate Planning

You get what you pay for

Like many things in life, the estate planning process is one of those situations where you truly get what you pay for.

Unfortunately, much of what passes for estate planning is little more than word processing. It's not uncommon for practitioners to have one or two "standard" forms that they use for every client, merely replacing names and dates. That is no way to plan your estate. After all, you're planning for everything you own and for everyone you love. That should make proper planning an important priority for every family.

If all you desire is word processing, why pay an attorney to do it? There are numerous resources on the Internet where you can download documents and fill in the names and information yourself! So why concern yourself with a comprehensive estate plan? Because there are often serious flaws in do-it-yourself form documents.

Standard forms often simplify everything to the point of absurdity. For example, instead of having specific guidelines for determining when you're disabled and instructions for how you should be cared for, the form document probably says you're disabled when a doctor says you are. Any doctor, whether they know you or not! And one doctor without a second opinion!

CHAPTER 50   The Cost of Estate Planning

When it comes to distributions, form documents simply say "divide it equally among all my children" and distribute it to them outright. What if your children are different ages, have different needs, or differ in their spending habits? What if they have marital problems or have been sued? The inheritance you leave in these situations may be immediately taken from them.

Many of the form documents do not include planning that will ensure that married couples take full advantage of the unlimited marital deduction AND their individual lifetime exemptions. Most are inadequate for planning for second and subsequent marriages where you have "her kids," "his kids," and "our kids."

> When it comes to estate planning, you get what you pay for. One client who came to us for a review of their Internet documents had accidentally disinherited their children!

Many form documents were copied from California (which is one of only nine community property states) or some other state's documents. And even though they are sold as "state specific" we often find important errors when reviewing documents that clients bring in for review.

One of the biggest problems is that the form trusts are rarely funded, so the whole estate ends up going through probate after death. The Forms-R-US company or word processing attorney made a little money selling you the word-processed form, but the real money comes from taking the estate through probate after you're gone.

The Internet form documents are cheap – there's no doubt about it! And even those form documents that are filled out by attorneys can be cheap. Comprehensive, thorough, counseling-centered estate planning is not cheap. But when you include after-death costs, the "cheap" form documents tend to end up costing much more overall.

To better understand the difference in costs and quality, there are several comparisons that can be made. The comprehensive estate planning is like building a custom home instead of a cheap tract house. Comprehensive estate

CHAPTER 50   The Cost of Estate Planning

planning is like the painting of a master instead of the velvet Elvis painting available in the truck stop gift shop.

One client, a big city Chief of Police, said it best: "When I'm shopping for bulletproof vests for my officers, my goal is not to find the cheapest one on the market."

Acknowledgements

The authors would like to acknowledge the members of their team who have contributed so greatly to this book:

- This book is dedicated to Rhonda Miller, Pat Bowman and Angela Christian, without whom it would not have been possible.

- In addition, we want to thank Randall Borkus who is a part of our advanced planning team.

- Cecil Smith and Carol Gonnella have been great partners for years in our work with Wyoming Close LLC's and Wyoming Domestic Asset Protection Trusts.

- We have greatly appreciated Larry Kendzior, author of *Conundrum: The Challenge of Execution in Middle-Market Companies* and his expertise in both valuations and explaining complex concepts to clients.

- Finally, this book would still be an idea if it were not for Dan Stuenzi. He's a great estate planner, publisher, editor, and friend.

APPENDIX A

Author Biographies

WILLIAM E. ANDERSEN

Attorney, Shareholder, Rated AV Preeminent

As the Founder and President of The Andersen Firm, Bill's objective is to develop lifelong relationships with his clients, not short-term engagements. Bill treats his clients as friends because friends can count on one another to do their very best. It is his goal and the goal of the firm to make the estate planning, estate settlement, estate litigation, asset protection and elder law as easy and comfortable as possible. There is no greater fulfillment than seeing clients smile and breathe a sigh of relief when their planning is in place. In addition to education, training, experience, and knowledge Bill has a reputation for being a good listener and for explaining concepts that might be confusing in a simple, straightforward manner without an abundance of "legalese."

Bill decided he wanted to be an attorney when he was only six years old. While growing up in East Tennessee, he had a family friend who was a prominent attorney and a great mentor. Bill graduated from the United States Military Academy at West Point where he received the Cleland Leadership Award. He was also elected by his fellow classmates to serve as the Chairman of the Honor Committee during the worst cheating scandal in West Point's history. He then went on to serve in the U.S. Army commanding infantry units in the 101st Airborne Division and Second U.S. Infantry Division in Korea. After his military service, he earned his J.D. at Vanderbilt University School of Law where he was Senior Managing Editor of the Vanderbilt Law Review. He later received his LL.M. in Estate Planning at the University Of Miami School Of Law.

Bill has been practicing law for almost 30 years and enjoys the AV Preeminent 5.0 out of 5.0 of Martindale Hubbell bestowed upon him by his peers and judges for ethical standards and legal knowledge. There is no higher rating that can be achieved. Other honors include serving as Deputy Assistant Secretary of Labor for Elizabeth Dole in the first Bush Administration, Republican Nominee for US

Senate in 1988, and being an appointee of former Florida Governor Jeb Bush to serve on the Judicial Nominating Committee for the 16th Judicial Circuit.

He is a member of the New York City Bar Association, Wealth Counsel, Union League Club of NYC and National Network of Estate Planning Attorneys as well as a member of the New York, Florida, District of Columbia and Tennessee Bars. Additionally, he has been appointed as an Accredited Estate Planner with the National Association of Estate Planners & Councils. He lectures frequently to individuals and groups and provides continuing education for other professionals.

Along with partners Jim Collins, Joleen Searles and Julie Ann Garber, Bill authored *The Pocket Guide to Trusts & Estates: Understanding Estate Planning, Estate Settlement, Estate Litigation, Asset Protection, and Elder Law*.

Bill's philosophy is to enjoy your life no matter what you are doing, at work and at play. When he's not working, you can catch him out fly fishing—both fresh and salt water - it's one of his favorite hobbies.

Licensed in: New York, District of Columbia, Florida, Tennessee

JAMES W. COLLINS

Attorney, Shareholder

James W. Collins is an Equity Partner in The Andersen Firm. Jim places a high premium on the value of client-specific counseling and design of a unique plan for each client that will ensure the client's estate plan works the way the client intends it to work, whether the client is alive and well, enduring a period of disability, or "looking down from a cloud" after life is over. The client in turn places a high premium on controlling, directing, and protecting assets during these same phases of life. The estate planning combination of clearly stated client goals and carefully counseled estate planning strategies becomes a powerful combination indeed.

Jim also practices in the related areas of probate and trust administration and elder law. He is an honors graduate of Thomas Cooley Law School in Lansing, Michigan and of the Esperti-Petersen Institute's Advanced Studies for Estate and Wealth Preservation.

Jim is licensed as an attorney in Florida and is a member of the American Bar Association (ABA), the Florida Bar, the Real Property, Probate and Trust Law section of the Florida Bar and the American Bar Association (ABA), the Elder Law section of the Florida Bar, the tax section of the American Bar Association (ABA), the Sarasota County Bar Association, the National Network of Estate Planning Attorneys, the National Academy of Elder Law Attorneys, WealthCounsel, LLC, and ElderCounsel, LLC. Jim is a nationally recognized speaker, and he teaches on a variety of topics, including (but not limited to) The Truth About Estate Planning, Planning With Certainty in Uncertain Times, Estate Plans That Work, Maximizing Your Retirement Plan Savings, Asset Protection in Florida, Spotting Advanced Planning Issues, The Truth About Tax Repeal, The Truth About Medicaid Planning, as well as workshops on topics such as minimizing the bite of estate tax, life insurance trusts (ILITs), charitable trusts, asset protection strategies, wealth preservation planning, business succession planning, and a variety of other advanced planning workshops.

Jim is the former Senior Faculty and Director of Legal Support for the National Network of Estate Planning Attorneys and a former faculty member for the Academy of Multidisciplinary Practice. He has served as an adjunct professor of business law for the University of South Florida, and has taught for InKnowVision, a high net worth planning collaborative and "think tank" in Chicago, Illinois. Along with partners William E. Andersen, Joleen Searles, and Julie Ann Garber, Jim authored *The Pocket Guide to Trusts & Estates: Understanding Estate Planning, Estate Settlement, Estate Litigation, Asset Protection, and Elder Law*.

Jim has been married to Susie since 1978 and has two children, Rebecca and Ben, as well as a grandson Liam. He enjoys fitness and distance running, especially marathoning and ultramarathoning. Jim has completed at least one marathon in each of the 50 states and D.C., and has run a number of "ultra marathons" as well, including the 100 mile distance. Jim's former background in ministry, both as senior pastor and college/seminary professor, strongly supports his counseling and relationship oriented practice as it focuses on estate plans that truly work.

JOLEEN SEARLES

Attorney, Shareholder

Joleen Searles is the managing attorney in The Andersen Firm's Tennessee Office. Joleen received her undergraduate degree from the University of Virginia and her J.D. from Hofstra University in Hempstead, New York. Ms. Searles then went on to earn an LL.M. (Advanced Law Degree) in Taxation from the University of Miami in Coral Gables.

Joleen is a member of The Tennessee Bar Association, The New York Bar Association, The Florida Bar Association and The American Bar Association. She focuses her practice in the areas of Estate Planning, Estate Settlement, Probate and Asset Protection.

Joleen frequently lectures on these topics, and others, during education presentations for Financial Advisors, CPAs, Insurance Brokers and other financial professionals as part of The Andersen Firm's Financial Advisor Continuing Education Program.

Along with partners William E. Andersen, Jim Collins and Julie Ann Garber, Joleen authored *The Pocket Guide to Trusts & Estates: Understanding Estate Planning, Estate Settlement, Estate Litigation, Asset Protection, and Elder Law.*

Joleen has lived in Texas, North Carolina, California, Japan, Alabama, Virginia, New York, Germany but has decided to make her home in Tennessee.

In her free time, Joleen enjoys going to the Theater and the Opera, traveling, watching and playing sports, wakeboarding, skiing and boating.

Attorney Searles is licensed in Florida, New York and Tennessee.

JULIE ANN GARBER, ESQ.

Attorney

Julie Ann Garber grew up in Pittsburgh, Pennsylvania, and earned a B.S. in Biology, graduating Magna Cum Laude, Phi Beta Kappa, from Allegheny College, in Meadville, PA, in 1988. After working as a toxicologist for a few years, Julie attended Duquesne University School of Law in Pittsburgh, PA, while working full-time as a molecular biologist. She earned her Juris Doctor in 1994.

Julie began practicing in the estate planning field in Maryland in 1995 and moved to Florida in 2004. She is an active member of the Florida Bar and the Maryland Bar and an inactive member of the Pennsylvania Bar.

Since 2008, Julie has been writing as the Guide to Wills & Estate Planning on *About.com*. She has written thousands of blogs and articles and updates and adds content on a weekly basis.

Julie is a co-author of *Estate Planning Strategies, Collective Wisdom, Proven Techniques* (Wealth Builders Press, 2009), as well as *Estate Planning Client Strategies* (Thomson/Reuters/Aspatore, 2011). She is also an ongoing contributor to the annually updated treatise Advising the Elderly Client (Thomson Reuters/West, 2013). Along with partners William E. Andersen, Jim Collins and Joleen Searles, Julie authored *The Pocket Guide to Trusts & Estates: Understanding Estate Planning, Estate Settlement, Estate Litigation, Asset Protection, and Elder Law*.

Julie's goal is to have each and every estate planning client fulfill their long-term wishes while upholding their values so that they leave her office with confidence that they've created a comprehensive estate plan that will work as anticipated when it is needed. She also strives to help her clients understand that estate planning is a lifelong process, not a one-time event to be rushed through during a stressful time.

ERIN L. TURNER

Director of Professional Alliances & Chief of Staff

When Erin Turner was growing up he had several positive mentors in his life – his dad, his business economics professor in college, and William Andersen, the founder of our firm. He went to Flagler College in St. Augustine and graduated with a Bachelor's Degree in Business Management with a minor in Marketing, Advertising and Market Research. Erin is licensed for Life, Health and Variable Annuity insurance in the state of Florida and has been approved by the Florida Department of Financial Services to instruct Continuing Education for 2-15 courses.

Erin grew up in the Jacksonville Beach area and today lives in Ft. Lauderdale- which is great because he always wanted to live in South Florida. When he's not working he loves to go surfing, play golf, fly airplanes, travel and ride motorcycles.

Working at The Andersen Firm for the past ten years has been a great experience for Erin. He really enjoys getting to know our diverse clients and working with financial planners and other referral sources to assist their clients in establishing a relationship with our firm. Erin is also lucky to be working with the remarkable group of people that are a part of The Andersen Firm. The greatest aspect of his work is to help ensure that all parties involved in a case are happy with our firm. If the clients are happy and our referral sources are happy and satisfied, then Erin feels he's done a good job – and that's what it's all about.

Erin's wish for every one of our clients is for them to realize that after they are gone, there is no way to make sure that their wishes are carried out without a proper estate plan. Putting everything in writing is necessary so the people you love won't have to deal with any unpleasant situations or lengthy court battles. Our firm is staffed by the most professional, highly-skilled attorneys and team members who are specialists in putting together solid estate plans and wills – we make the process easy and comfortable.

JERRY SARESKY

Chief Paralegal

As the firm's Chief Paralegal, attention to detail and precise implementation of our clients' intentions are Jerry's ultimate goals. He takes pride in proofing or drafting each and every document as if it were his own. Jerry recognizes that no two individuals are the same, that each family is a world of its own. As such, each plan is unique to each client, and Jerry can be trusted to not only erect the foundations of the estate or asset protection plan, but also to craft the meticulous details that make the plan a perfect fit. Jerry also understands how vital it is to listen to all the parties involved in the design such as other trusted advisors, CPAs, lawyers, financial advisors, and anyone else who our client believes can contribute to the plan design and creation.

Jerry Saresky acquired his expertise in the Estate Planning and Asset Protection areas over his twelve year career with The Andersen Firm. This consistency allowed him to move through many different positions in the organization, learning vital skills in each step. This makes Jerry a very complete paralegal, able to assist clients and attorneys with basic and advanced estate planning techniques, at both a conceptual and detailed level.

Jerry has been issued a Florida Registered Paralegal certification by the Florida Bar in 2008. He attended Florida Atlantic University where he earned his Bachelor's Degree with highest honors in business administration with an emphasis in accounting. This education enabled Jerry to gain an understanding of our clients' finances, business operations, and the overwhelming complexities of the federal tax code. Jerry is also a member of Phi Kappa Phi and Golden Key academic honor societies, and he is now on his way to becoming an attorney.

Along with attorneys William E. Andersen, Joleen Searles, Jim Collins, and Julie Ann Garber, Jerry authored *The Pocket Guide to Trusts & Estates: Understanding Estate Planning, Estate Settlement, Estate Litigation, Asset Protection, and Elder Law*.

Jerry is married to Astrid and a dedicated father to his beautiful daughter Lilli. Prior to joining The Andersen Firm, Jerry started and operated a chain of small retail stores in his home city, Buenos Aires.

APPENDIX B

SUMMARY OF KEY IDEAS

Do you have the Seven Mandatory Components of a Foundational Estate Plan?

1. **Revocable Living Trust**
   This instrument contains in-depth instructions for your care if you become mentally disabled, and the care of your loved ones upon your passing. Furthermore, it efficiently transfers your property to your loved ones at the time of your death, avoiding probate and allowing for the maximum utilization of estate tax exemptions.

2. **Pour Over Will**
   Upon your death, your pour-over will leaves any property to your living trust that you did not retitle before your death. It functions as a safety net to make sure any property you neglected to place in your trust can ultimately be managed by your Trustees pursuant to your instructions.

3. **Durable Power of Attorney**
   A durable power of attorney allows someone else to handle financial matters for assets in your individual name, particularly retirement plans. It is also used to put assets in your trust if you become mentally disabled prior to your trust becoming fully funded.

4. **Living Will**
   This instrument directs your physician as to whether or not to cease life-sustaining procedures which would serve only to prolong your death if you are terminally ill. It gives guidelines for your physician to follow, as well as clarifies your intent as to life-sustaining procedures.

5. **Health Care Surrogate / Health Care Power of Attorney**
   This instrument designates a health care surrogate or health care power of attorney if you are incapable of making health care decisions or providing informed consent. It must also account for HIPAA (Health Insurance Portability and Accountability Act) of 1996 to be effective.

6. **Quitclaim Bill of Sale**
   This instrument places your personal property (e.g. furniture and jewelry) into your trust, thus avoiding the need to probate your personal property.

7. **Funding**
   Most assets will need to be retitled into the trust to make the trust effective for disability planning and to avoid probate. Funding a trust is just as important as creating the trust.

To arrange for a complimentary review of your estate plan, please call us at:

866.230.2206

© 2013, The Andersen Firm, A Professional Corporation

SUMMARY OF KEY IDEAS

Benefits of the IRA Inheritance Trust

1. **Ensure "Stretch-out"**

   With the tax law change in 2003, the IRS allows the required minimum distributions (RMDs) of inherited IRAs to be calculated using the beneficiaries' life expectancy. What this means is smaller distributions and longer tax free compounding. Unfortunately, most inherited IRAs never get to enjoy this "stretch" because the IRA is "blown". This "blow-out" happens either because the beneficiaries don't understand the rules or they just want to spend it. The IRA Inheritance Trust allows you to lockup the IRA and ensure the stretch while still allowing the beneficiary access to those funds should they need them in an emergency.

2. **Divorce Protection**

   IRAs should not be included in a divorce decree. However, going through a divorce is a very stressful time and IRAs are frequently seen by divorce attorneys as a easily accessible pot of money to fund a marital dissolution agreement. The IRA Inheritance Trust will protect against a beneficiary losing the inherited IRA through a divorce.

3. **Protection for Minors**

   People are apprehensive about leaving money to minors because they do not know how that person will grow up and do not want to fund self-destructive habits. With the IRA Inheritance Trust you can name a trustee that ensures that the assets are there for the minors' benefit but will not be used to exacerbate any character flaws.

4. **Lawsuit, Creditor, and Bankruptcy Protection**

   Inherited IRAs should be protected from these types of claims but when the money is withdrawn from the IRA, as most beneficiaries do, those funds are subject to the claims of creditors and bankruptcy. With the IRA Inheritance Trust you can protect not only the corpus of the IRA but also the required minimum distributions.

5. **Protection from Losing Government Benefits**

   For those individuals who receive government benefits any asset left in an inheritance can be subject to the payback rules. With the IRA Inheritance Trust you can be certain that those monies will be used to give that beneficiary the "extras" in life and not be used to pay back Uncle Sam.

6. **Minimize Future Estate Taxes**

   If IRA assets are left to beneficiaries in their individual name they may be subject to estate taxes when they pass as the inherited IRA is includable in the beneficiaries' estate. However, if the IRA is left in the IRA Inheritance Trust it will never be estate taxable again.

7. **Leave a Legacy in Your Name**

   Eventually we are all going to pass on to our greater glory. It is how we are remembered by those who loved us and knew us that keeps us alive forever. With the IRA Inheritance Trust a check will be coming to your beneficiaries with your name on it for their benefit every quarter. This will be part of your legacy.

To arrange for a complimentary review of your estate plan, please call us at:

866.230.2206

© 2013, The Andersen Firm, A Professional Corporation

SUMMARY OF KEY IDEAS

Three Options for Estate Planning

1. **Foundational Planning**

   Every client needs Foundational Planning. This planning includes the "Seven Mandatory Components of an Estate Plan" (e.g. revocable living trust, pour-over will, financial power of attorney, health care surrogate, living will, quitclaim bill of sale, and a funding plan). It also includes state-of-the-art asset protection for the surviving spouse and children. In addition, Foundational Planning may include Generation Skipping Transfer Tax planning to avoid a degree of estate tax in subsequent generations and an IRA Inheritance Trust to provide asset protection and achieve other goals as the client passes retirement plan assets to beneficiaries.

2. **Advanced Planning**

   Once the Foundational elements of an estate plan are in place, Advanced Planning then builds on that by focusing on specific solutions to the client's specific objectives, challenges, and planning issues. As such, it is an "a la carte" approach that provides planning choices to meet client goals. Advanced Planning often employs techniques such as sophisticated IRA Inheritance Trusts (IRAITs), advanced Generation Skipping Transfer Tax planning (GSTT), Irrevocable Life Insurance Trusts (ILITs), Buildup Equity Retirement Trusts (BERTs, aka Spousal Gifting Trusts), Qualified Personal Residence Trusts (QPRTs), Legacy Trusts (Gifting Trusts for beneficiaries other than spouses), Limited Liability Companies, Asset Protection Planning, a degree of Asset Gifting Strategies, basic Charitable Remainder Trusts (CRTs), Special/Supplemental Needs Trusts for special needs beneficiaries (SNTs), etc. This list is not meant to be exhaustive, but rather illustrative of some of the tools we employ at this level.

3. **Global Planning**

   Global Planning requires personal and financial analysis which leads to "modeling," i.e., a customized design for each client. This cash flow analysis and modeling is designed to ensure that both the immediate and long-term consequences of Global Planning meet the client's needs and goals. There are no time-frame limitations placed on Global Planning as it is anticipated that the client/firm relationship and the planning will continue for the long-term as the plan is implemented and maintained to achieve client goals.

   For a client to be willing to engage in Global Planning, they have to be comfortable with a long-term relationship, willing to engage the legal services to carry it out, and prepared to tolerate some additional and necessary complexity. Global Planning is about bringing a very high level of value and service to the client and their estate planning.

To arrange for a complimentary review of
your estate plan, please call us at:

866.230.2206

© 2013, The Andersen Firm, A Professional Corporation

SUMMARY OF KEY IDEAS

Uncle Sam's 6 Options for Paying the Estate Tax

1. **Pay the Tax**

    This is the option that Uncle Sam wants you to choose and is the default option if you do not choose any of the other 5 options. Upon the second spouse's death any amount over and above the federal exemption amount will be subject to a tax. This also is true for any amount over and above the state exemption amounts depending on the state you are a resident of.

2. **Spend it All**

    Spending down the estate by taking long vacations buying more expensive cars, eating out at fancy restaurants is a way to avoid paying the estate tax. However, this option does not appeal to most people who have worked their entire lives to obtain the wealth they have.

3. **Gift it to Charity**

    Gifting any amounts over the current exemption amount to a charity(ies) will negate any federal estate tax. However, for most of us charity starts at home and we would rather see those monies go to our children and beneficiaries.

4. **Gift it to Beneficiaries**

    A gifting program properly implemented and adhered to is a great way to pass wealth down to beneficiaries and out of the estate. However, the gifting program must have enough time to make an impact and will not be effective if it is started late in life.

5. **Advanced Planning Techniques**

    There are over 60 different estate planning techniques that can zero out estate taxes no matter how large the estate. These techniques, while effective, will add a level of complexity that many people simply do not want to deal with.

6. **Irrevocable Life Insurance Trust**

    The irrevocable life insurance trust or ILIT is a special type of trust, that is the owner and the beneficiary of, a special type of insurance. The insurance inside this trust is guaranteed level premium, guaranteed benefit and can be placed on the life of one spouse or both spouses. The payout from the policy is not estate taxable and is specifically earmarked to pay the estate taxes. This option is the simplest and cleanest way to deal with the estate tax.

To arrange for a complimentary review of your estate plan, please call us at:

866.230.2206

© 2013, The Andersen Firm, A Professional Corporation

SUMMARY OF KEY IDEAS

Advanced Techniques for Estate Planning

1. **Qualified Personal Residence Trust (QPRT)**
   The QPRT allows you to move your primary or secondary residence out of your taxable estate while still allowing you to retain complete possession and use of the residence. After your passing the home is then transferred to your intended beneficiaries. This technique, while effective at reducing your taxable estate, can become complicated if you wish to sell the property in the trust.

2. **Buildup Equity Retirement Trust (BERT)**
   The BERT is an estate tax sheltered irrevocable trust that is set up by each spouse for the benefit of the other spouse. Gifts are made to the trust annually and, while still accessible, the assets are exempt from gift tax and estate tax. Also, because the trust is irrevocable the assets are protected from creditors and predators. Then upon the spouse's death the assets are passed on to intended beneficiaries.

3. **Irrevocable Life Insurance Trust (ILIT)**
   The irrevocable life insurance trust or ILIT is a special type of trust, that holds and is the beneficiary of, a special type of insurance. This insurance inside this trust is guaranteed level premium, guaranteed benefit and can be placed on the life of one spouse or both spouses. The payout from the policy is not estate taxable and is specifically earmarked to pay the estate taxes.

4. **Limited Liability Companies (LLC)**
   An LLC is a business entity formed under the laws of specific states and are commonly used for estate compression for tax purposes and asset protection. Shareholders or "Members" of the LLC cannot be personally liable for the debts of the LLC. Also, the assets that are owned by the LLC can be "compressed" and used for wealth transfer.

5. **Grantor Retained Annuity Trust (GRAT)**
   A GRAT is an irrevocable trust in which the grantor transfers assets into the trust and retains the right to annual payments of a fixed amount of principal and interest for a prescribed number of years. At the end of the period the assets go to the beneficiaries in accordance with the grantor's intentions.

6. **Legacy Trust**
   A Legacy Trust is an irrevocable lifetime gifting trust established and funded while the grantor is alive. The assets in the trust are there for the benefit of the kids but are asset protected from the claims of creditors, predators (lawsuits) and divorcing spouses.

7. **Grantor Deemed Owner Trust (GDOT)**
   A GDOT is an irrevocable trust used to "freeze" the value of estate assets for estate and gift tax purposes by selling an asset to the trust in exchange for a promissory note. These trusts are also commonly referred to as Intentionally Defective Grantor Trusts (IDGTs).

To arrange for a complimentary review of your estate plan, please call us at:

866.230.2206

© 2013, The Andersen Firm, A Professional Corporation

SUMMARY OF KEY IDEAS

Asset Protection Planning

1. **Goal of Asset Protection Planning**

   The goal of asset protection planning is to change a creditor's economic analysis. In order to properly understand asset protection, one must analyze timing, the creditor, and the specific assets under consideration.

2. **Not About Hiding Assets**

   Asset protection is not about hiding assets. It doesn't work. Private investigators may find the assets. They will be found out in a debtor examination. Perjuring oneself is not a viable option.

3. **Concepts**

   The first concept of asset protection is that creditors can only go after assets that you actually own. The strategy is to remove title of the asset from the client's name but still allow them to have control and enjoyment of those assets. The way we do this is through limited liability companies and through trusts. With respect to certain limited liability companies, there is no remedy to attach a membership interest. In certain states, the only thing a creditor can obtain is a charging order. The creditor cannot force a distribution. Thus, it makes it difficult for the creditor to get to the asset. This makes settlement much more favorable to the debtor. The second concept is certain assets are exempt depending on the State. For example, Texas, Kansas, Florida, and Nevada have desirable homestead protection. In other States, like Florida, annuities and life insurance are protected by statute and court decision. The third concept is to make assets less desirable. An example of this would be placing liens on real estate. For example, one could create a home equity line of credit from a family member and secure it with a deed of trust.

4. **Better To Do Something**

   It is generally better to do something rather than do nothing. If you do nothing it is almost certain that you will lose the asset. If you do something, you have a much better chance of keeping all or part of the assets.

5. **Fraudulent Transfers**

   One must carefully consider whether a court will view a transfer as a fraudulent conveyance to defraud creditors.

6. **Estate Planning and Financial Planning**

   Asset protection is frequently and best done as part of and in the context of an overall estate plan and financial plan.

To arrange for a complimentary review of
your estate plan, please call us at:

866.230.2206

© 2013, The Andersen Firm, A Professional Corporation

Estate Litigation

The estate litigation attorneys at The Andersen Firm represent beneficiaries, trustees and personal representatives in various jurisdictions dealing with estate litigation and probate litigation matters.

A will contest challenges the admission of a will to probate or seeks to revoke the probate of a will that is already pending before the probate court.

A similar type of estate litigation can take place contesting the terms of a trust. The most common causes of action in both will contests and estate litigation follow.

1. **Lack of Capacity**

    Under the law, a testator is required to have mental competency to make a last will and testament or trust and to understand the nature of his or her estate assets and the people to whom the estate assets are going to be distributed. A will or trust can be declared void if lack of capacity can be proven. Usually, incompetence is established through a prior medical diagnosis of dementia, senility, Alzheimer's or psychosis.

2. **Undue Influence**

    When the testator is compelled or coerced to execute a will or trust as a result of improper pressure exerted on him or her, by a relative, friend, trusted advisor, or health care worker, a cause of action arises. In many cases, the undue influencer will upset a long established estate plan where the bulk of the estate was to pass to the descendants or close relatives of the decedent. In other cases, one child of the decedent will coerce the decedent to write the other children out of the will or trust.

3. **Lack of Formalities**

    Proper execution of a last will and testament or trust requires that the will or trust be signed by the testator and witnessed and signed by two unrelated parties. A last will and testament can be contested on the basis that it was not properly drafted, signed, or witnessed in accordance with the law.

4. **Breach of Fiduciary Duty**

    The personal representative of an estate or the trustee of a trust owes the beneficiaries of the estate or trust certain fiduciary duties including but not limited to honesty, prudence and loyalty. When those duties are violated by a trustee or personal representative, a cause of action arises.

5. **Elective Share**

    Some states provide an elective share to surviving spouses, which provides the surviving spouse with a portion of the deceased spouse's estate according to a statutory formula. Deadlines may be associated to make the elective share.

6. **Forged Documents**

    Documents can be forged to create unintentional outcomes with the intent to deceive. When documents appear altered or falsified, a cause of action arises.

To arrange for a complimentary review of your estate plan, please call us at:

866.230.2206

© 2013, The Andersen Firm, A Professional Corporation

SUMMARY OF KEY IDEAS

Probate and Trust Settlement

The following is a summary of the steps to be taken when settling an estate or trust. The person responsible for settling an estate is called the PERSONAL REPRESENTATIVE ("PR") and the person responsible for settling a trust is called a SUCCESSOR TRUSTEE ("Trustee").

1. **Inventory of Documents and Finances**

   The PR or Trustee should locate all original estate planning documents and any additional written instructions the decedent may have left.

2. **Appointing a Personal Representative**

   If assets are owned outside a trust, probate documents need to be filed with the appropriate court in the county where the decedent resided at the time of death to appoint a PR to oversee the disposition of the estate. If assets titled in individual name are located in another state, an ancillary probate may be necessary.

3. **Obtain EIN and Open Bank Account**

   The PR must obtain a taxpayer identification number for the estate and open an estate checking account for use in holding estate assets and paying estate debts. The Trustee must obtain a taxpayer identification number for the decedent's trust and notify the decedent's bank that he or she is the Successor Trustee of the decedent's trust.

4. **Give Notice to Beneficiaries**

   The PR must forward the Notice of Administration to all beneficiaries. In some states, the PR must send a complete copy of the will to beneficiaries. If the decedent did not leave a will, the PR must send a copy of the Letters of Administration to each heir.

5. **Payments of Expenses**

   The Clerk will publish a notice in the local newspaper to notify any unknown creditors of the decedent's death.

6. **File Documents with Court**

   The PR must file an inventory of the decedent's estate assets within 60 days of appointment unless waived by the will or by consent of residual beneficiaries.

7. **Payment of Taxes**

   The PR or Trustee must determine if any federal and/or state estate tax returns will need to be filed and, if taxes are due, how the taxes will be paid. Estate tax returns are due 9 months after the decedent's date of death.

8. **Distribution of Assets**

   The PR or Trustee must make the final distribution of the decedent's property and obtain receipts from the beneficiaries. The PR must file all required closing documents with the Court to close the estate.

To arrange for a complimentary review of your estate plan, please call us at:

866.230.2206

© 2013, The Andersen Firm, A Professional Corporation

SUMMARY OF KEY IDEAS

Elder Law

1. The Focus of Elder Law

This area of the law concentrates on counseling senior citizens, persons with disabilities, and their families, while emphasizing the highest quality of care for the individual in need. Elder Law planning may be right for you, or may be a perfect fit for your parents, family members, or loved ones even if your personal planning takes you in a different direction.

2. Planning for Your Long Term Health Care

Some studies have indicated that you have a nearly 50% chance of a "long term care episode" once you are beyond the age of 65. Your options for paying for this care are largely limited to investing in long term care insurance, privately paying for your care, Medicare and Medicare Supplement insurance, Medicaid benefits and Veterans Administration (VA) benefits. It makes all the difference in the world for you to be proactive in planning for your long term health care before your options are taken away from you.

3. Medicare and Medicaid

It is critical that you understand the differences between Medicare SSDI (Social Security Disability Insurance), Medicaid, SSI (Supplemental Security Income), and more. We find that there is much confusion here, and that often clients are not receiving the full advantage of help they are entitled to or could qualify for.

4. Veterans Benefits

If you have served the United States in some branch of the military(Thank You!), you or your surviving spouse or family may be entitled to Service Related Disability Benefits, and/or Veterans' Pension Benefits. Too often, we meet veterans who are struggling to make ends meet and are completely unaware of the help that is available to them in this arena.

5. Special Needs Trusts

This planning is also known as "Supplemental Needs Trusts" planning, often abbreviated as SNT planning. If an individual with special needs receives assets in their own name, often as the resultof a lawsuit or settlement, good planning with a self-settled or first party SNT can make sure their benefit from those funds is structured so that they can qualify or continue to qualify for government benefits. Alternatively, parents or grandparents (or others) often fund an SNT with their own assets for the benefit of their disabled loved one. The nuances in this planning are important.

6. And Much More!

Effective Elder Law planning also pays careful attention to and provides counseling in essential estate planning, cases of elder abuse, elder fraud, living arrangements, securing appropriate financial planning, and any other application of the law to senior citizens, persons with disabilities, and their families.

To arrange for a complimentary review of
your estate plan, please call us at:

866.230.2206

© 2013, The Andersen Firm, A Professional Corporation

The Andersen Firm
Attorneys at Law
A Professional Corporation

ESTATE PLANNING • ESTATE SETTLEMENT • ESTATE LITIGATION
ASSET PROTECTION • ELDER LAW
PHONE: 866.230.2206 | FAX: 877.733.1433 | WWW.THEANDERSENFIRM.COM

William E. Andersen

New York Office
110 E. 37th Street
New York, NY 10016
Tel: 866.230.2206
Fax: 877.773.1433

Washington DC Office
601 Pennsylvania Avenue NW
Suite 900 South Building
Washington, DC 20004
Tel: 866.230.2206
Fax: 877.773.1433

Northern Virginia Office
8300 Boone Boulevard
Suite 500
Vienna, VA 22182
Tel: 866.230.2206
Fax: 877.773.1433

South Florida Office
500 E. Broward Blvd.
Suite 1600
Fort Lauderdale, FL 33394
Tel: 866.230.2206
Fax: 877.773.1433

West Florida Office
7273 Bee Ridge Road
Sarasota, FL 34241
Tel: 866.230.2206
Fax: 877.773.1433

Southwest Florida Office
23150 Fashion Drive
Suite 232
P.O. Box 1240
Estero, FL 33928/33929
Tel: 866.230.2206
Fax: 877.773.1433

Tennessee Office
862 Med Tech Parkway
Suite 200
Johnson City, TN 37604
Tel: 866.230.2206
Fax: 877.773.1433

Florida Keys Office
422 Fleming Street
Key West, FL 33040
Tel: 866.230.2206
Fax: 877.773.1433